"This is a deep, rich, profoundly ~~~~ ~p~~ preparing for marriage as a lifelong vocation and who want theirs to last. But it's also a great on-going resource for the already-married. Wonderfully organized and written, and highly recommended."

—Most. Rev. Charles J. Chaput, O.F.M. Cap.
Archbishop of Philadelphia

"Grounded in solid Catholic theology, attractively presented, and helpfully seasoned with real-life examples from married life, *One Body* provides readers with a healthy and holy appreciation of the gifts of a generous and happily-married couple. The seven lessons can serve as a great resource for parish study groups."

—Most Reverend Joseph E. Kurtz, D.D.
Archbishop of Louisville

"With great vigor, Pope Francis has reminded us of the need to accompany spouses and those considering marriage along their journeys. . . . There is much to be gained by the small groups or couples who utilize this sound and practical work!"

—Curtis Martin
Founder and President,
Fellowship of Catholic University Students (FOCUS)

"What I love about this book is its blend of intelligence and heart. It marshals the best that the Church has to offer in the way of Scripture and theology, while integrating this seamlessly with the emotional and psychological features of marriage."

—Helen Alvaré
Professor, George Mason University of Law

ONE
BODY

ONE BODY

A Program of Marriage Preparation
and Enrichment for the New
Evangelization

John and Claire Grabowski

EMMAUS
ROAD
PUBLISHING

www.EmmausRoad.org
Steubenville, Ohio

Emmaus Road Publishing
1468 Parkview Circle
Steubenville, Ohio 43952

2018 John and Claire Grabowski
All rights reserved. Published 2018
Printed in the United States of America

Library of Congress Cataloging-in-Publication Data
Names: Grabowski, John S., author.
Title: One body : a program of marriage preparation and enrichment for the
  new evangelization / John Grabowski, Claire Grabowski.
Description: Steubenville : Emmaus Road, 2018.
Identifiers: LCCN 2017056616 (print) | LCCN 2017058396 (ebook) | ISBN
  9781947792593 (ebook) | ISBN 9781947792579 (hard cover) | ISBN
  9781947792586 (pbk.)
Subjects: LCSH: Marriage--Religious aspects--Catholic Church--Textbooks.
Classification: LCC BX2250 (ebook) | LCC BX2250 .G68 2018 (print) | DDC
  259/.13--dc23
LC record available at https://lccn.loc.gov/2017056616

Cover image: © MNStudio / Shutterstock.com
Cover design and layout by Margaret Ryland

CONTENTS

*For the many couples who have
allowed us to accompany them before
and after their weddings.*

INTRODUCTION

The Need for This Book:
New Challenges for a Lifelong Vocation

Like the priesthood and consecrated religious life, the Church sees marriage as a lifelong vocation entered by making irrevocable promises. Yet while men and women preparing for these religious vocations might spend ten years or more undergoing intensive preparation through study, prayer, community life, and pastoral ministry, for centuries men and women entering marriage did so with no explicit formation except the catechesis they had received as children and young adults and a brief interview with a priest to make sure that they met the requirements for marriage established by canon law.

Recognizing the need to do more, the Catholic Church in the United States and throughout the world has instituted longer and more formal programs of marriage preparation which can span a period of some six to twelve months before the wedding. In spite of these programs and the fact that in the United States Catholic marriage preparation or "pre-Cana" programs are among the best available among Christian churches and communities, the consensus among both the Church's pastors and those in marriage ministry is that we have to do more to prepare couples and we have to do it better. Furthermore, married couples need ongoing formation and support after their wedding as they seek to live out their vocation.

This does not mean that we are suggesting that engaged or married couples enter something like a seminary or religious community for multiple years of preparation before or after they marry. One of the things that sets the vocation of marriage apart from holy orders and vocations to religious life is that it is lived "in the world" in a more direct way and so withdrawal from the world is not an option or goal.

But, the world in which marriage is lived is changing. There are new challenges facing marriage today that our parents and grandparents did not face (such as technological control of human fertility, cybersex, questions about whether only men and women can marry) or did not face to the same extent (such as widespread materialism, cohabitation, or a "culture of divorce" which dissuades people from marrying). Recent popes such as Blessed Paul VI, Saint John Paul II, and Benedict XVI have spoken of the dark forces opposing the vocation of marriage in our day as a kind of "anti-civilization" or a "culture of death." Pope Francis has spoken of a "crisis" of the family impacted by individualism and con- sumerism[1] or "a culture of the ephemeral" where people move from one relationship to the next.[2]

But every new challenge the Church faces is also a new opportunity. Recent popes have also called for a "New Evangelization"—an evangeliza- tion which would not just carry the Gospel to those who have not heard of Christ, but would transform the lives of persons in places where Chris- tian faith was once strong, but is fading (such as Europe and, increasingly, the United States). In 2011, Pope Benedict XVI created a new pontifi- cal council to aid the Church in carrying out this task. Pope Francis has made this effort the focus of his ministry, inviting all of the members of the Church to live as "missionary disciples" who are "actively engaged in evangelization" (EG 120).

This challenge and opportunity for the whole Church is also given to those preparing for marriage, those living it out, and those who accom- pany them in this process. Marriage formation has to be, above all, an

---

[1] See Pope Francis, Apostolic Exhortation on the Proclamation of the Gospel in Today's World *Evangelii gaudium* (November 24, 2013), §66 (hereafter cited in the text as EG). All Church documents cited in this work can be found on the Vatican English website: http://w2.vatican.va/content/vatican/en.html.

[2] Pope Francis, Post-Synodal Apostolic Exhortation on Love in the Family *Amoris lae- titia* (March 19, 2016), §39 (hereafter cited in the text as AL).

opportunity and occasion to encounter the Person of Christ and His transforming love. It is from Him that the Sacrament of Marriage derives its power to sustain a couple in living out their promises of love and fidelity in the face of an increasingly hostile culture. Therefore, marriage formation is always geared toward evangelization. In our day it must be at the service of the New Evangelization.

This is not only true for persons who are not from a Christian background or baptized persons who are not practicing their faith. Every person, no matter his or her degree of faith, should be given the opportunity to encounter anew or for the first time the person of Jesus Christ. This opportunity should come through invitation—and not from any form of coercion. Like the first disciples inviting their family and friends to meet the Rabbi who was like no other, those engaged in the ministry of marriage preparation have the opportunity to ask others to "come and see" (see Jn 1:46) the One who has transformed their lives. As Pope Francis puts it in his 2013 Apostolic Exhortation *Evangelii gaudium* (*The Joy of the Gospel*): "I invite all Christians, everywhere, at this very moment, to a renewed personal encounter with Jesus Christ, or at least an openness to letting him encounter them; I ask all of you to do this unfailingly each day" (EG 3).

But even for those who have encountered Christ, there is always the opportunity to go deeper in their faith. Marriage formation should also be an opportunity to understand more fully the gift of marriage, which the Letter to the Ephesians calls "a great mystery" (see Eph 5:32). This is true for those undergoing marriage formation as well as for those offering it. Hence, marriage formation is also always a form of catechesis—life-shaping instruction in the truth of Christian faith. Effective catechesis always joins truth and life. It is the witness of lives based on and changed by the truth of the Gospel that authenticates the words shared in the proclamation of the New Evangelization.

Where This Book Fits in the Process of Marriage Formation

Catechesis is a process of formation that takes place over the whole of one's life. Based on this awareness, the Church has increasingly recognized instruction regarding marriage as a part of this formation process rather than something that takes place immediately before a wedding.

Pope St. John Paul II, in his Apostolic Exhortation *Familiaris consortio* (*On the Role of the Christian Family*, 1981), spoke of three stages of preparation for the vocation of marriage—remote, proximate, and immediate.[3] Increasingly, the Church and its pastors are recognizing the need for continuing support and formation of couples beyond the point of their wedding. Pope Francis has very explicitly called for an intensive accompaniment of couples in their first years of married life (see AL 217–30).

Remote preparation begins in the earliest years of a child's life. Through it the child learns the basic truths of human existence: the dignity and value of human beings (including themselves), the nature of love, the meaning of good and evil, the nature of truth, the need for forgiveness, and the reality of sex differences. He or she also learns the basic truths of Christian faith—the reality of God, creation, and sin, as well as our salvation in Jesus Christ, the power of the Holy Spirit, and the mystery of the Church. This foundation in human values and Christian faith prepares the child for later making a gift of him- or herself in love, whether in marriage or in priesthood or in consecrated religious life.

Proximate preparation for marriage is given as the child matures and takes part more fully in the Church's life. Usually this is given in the context of preparing for the Sacraments of Reconciliation, Eucharist, and Confirmation. Part of this formation should be deeper instruction in Christian moral living, including sexual morality, marriage, and the nature of family life—this instruction should take place in cooperation

---

[3] See Pope St. John Paul II, Apostolic Exhortation on the Role of the Christian Family in the Modern World *Familiaris consortio* (November 22, 1981), §66 (hereafter cited in the text as FC).

with the parents and in an age-appropriate manner, providing the basis for the young person's discernment of God's call regarding his or her future state of life. [4]

Immediate preparation is given to those who have determined that they are called to marriage and are in the process of preparing to wed. Such programs or courses, Pope John Paul II said, must provide a blend of information concerning marriage—"doctrinal, pedagogical, legal, and medical." But they must do this in a way that enables those taking part to gain "a deeper knowledge of the mystery of Christ and the Church" and "a desire to enter actively into the ecclesial community" (FC 66). This book is aimed at providing this kind of immediate preparation for engaged couples.

Ongoing formation refers to teaching and support offered to couples beyond their wedding as they live out their marital vocation. Such "post-Cana" formation is perhaps the greatest need of the Church in regard to its ministry to marriage in our day. It is aimed at helping couples to understand the commitment they have made and to develop the skills needed to live it out. However, those engaged in such ministry often struggle with a dearth of effective resources as well as models for how they might be used. This book can also be profitably used to provide this kind of ongoing formation for those in the early stages of their marriage or those married for some time who want to understand their vocation more deeply and live it more intentionally.

How to Use This Book

As a tool for marriage formation, this book is designed to be used in both small group and couple-to-couple formats. It can be used in parishes or larger diocesan settings as well, provided that there are a sufficient

---

[4] A wonderful resource in this process of formation for parents and religious educators is the Pontifical Council for the Family's 1995 document *The Truth and Meaning of Human Sexuality* available online at http://www.vatican.va/roman_curia/pontifical_councils/family/documents/rc_pc_family_doc_08121995_human-sexuality_en.html.

number of mentor couples to break the class into small groups and facilitate discussion within them. Four or five couples are an ideal size for such small groups, as higher numbers make discussion unwieldy and do not allow time for everyone to share.

The program envisions at least seven sessions to cover the material. These sessions can be spread over seven months if there is sufficient time, but they can also be held as often as every two weeks if the schedule is more compressed. Because the sessions build on individual study of texts and couples sharing outside of the context of the meetings (what we call "homework"), we do not recommend trying to hold them on a weekly basis. We strongly recommend that at least one of these sessions include a meal—either shared at the home of the mentor couple if done in a couple-to-couple format, or a potluck if this book is used in a group setting. The Scripture study chapters or one of the topics described in the appendices could also be the basis of individual sessions, providing enough material for a twelve-week formation course conducted in a parish setting.

This program should be used with the assistance and oversight of priests of the parish or diocese. When used for marriage preparation, it is usually necessary for a priest to meet individually with each engaged couple in order to interview them to ensure that they meet the requirements for marriage set forth in canon law as articulated by the local diocese. Using this program does not remove the need for such a canonical inquiry. Priests can also assist with selecting mentor couples, ensuring that they have the necessary formation to undertake this ministry. Many parishes and dioceses have training programs for those who want to serve as mentor couples. In addition, priests can also serve as resources for the couples involved, providing information and insight on questions that might emerge during discussion sessions so that mentor couples do not feel that they have to "have all the answers."

In addition to working with the Church's pastoral ministers, those who serve as mentor couples should themselves also embody an authentic pastoral spirit. They do not need to be experts in theology or psychology, and they are certainly not there because their own marriages or lives are perfect. Rather, they are there to share their own experience of the challenges and joys of living the vocation of marriage as taught by the Church. The Church's teaching can be challenging or difficult, but it embodies a call to conversion and a continual offer of God's mercy when couples fall short of it.[5] Approaching this ministry in this spirit, mentor couples find that their own marriages are strengthened. This has been our consistent experience in over 25 years of marriage ministry.

The book is written with various "layers" of information provided. The Scripture texts and brief commentaries as well as the catechetical overviews are meant to be prayerfully studied by everyone. Couples (teaching or mentor couples as well as those undergoing formation) should also answer the study and reflection questions prior to their sessions together. Couples are encouraged to share their answers with each other before and after sessions. The idea for everyone taking part is to encourage and deepen communication on topics vital to their marriages (future or present). There are also additional background readings focused on Scripture provided for each session that form the basis for the catechetical overviews. Couples receiving formation will find these helpful in gaining a deeper understanding of the ideas presented and discussed in the sessions. Mentor or teaching couples are strongly encouraged to work through these texts, enhancing their own ongoing formation as well as their ability to guide discussion. There are also a number of brief appendices provided with additional topics which can be introduced in the final session or treated in a separate session according to the specific needs of individual couples or groups.

Life is always busy and the months leading up to or following a wedding are exceptionally so. But we have found that the more time and effort couples are able to devote to preparing for their marriage, the more they benefit. Notice that we said preparing for marriage—not the wedding. A wedding lasts a part of a day. A marriage is meant to last a

---

[5] Pope John Paul II calls this process of continual conversion and discovery of God's mercy "the law of gradualness" and he contrasts it with a false pastoral approach that seeks to undermine or change challenging points of the Church's teaching ("the gradualness of the law"). See *Familiaris consortio*, §9.

lifetime. Many couples reverse this order by spending all of their time and energy (and money!) on planning a wedding rather than preparing for their life together. God is the primary actor in the covenant and Sacrament of Marriage, and He abundantly blesses the time and effort couples devote to preparing for living this vocation. So we encourage those using this program to be generous in the time they devote to it.

The format of study texts and sessions reflect our own experience of "best practices" in working with couples. We have found that couples benefit from pondering Scripture texts and discussion questions ahead of time. This enables them to see the connections between Scripture and the Church's vision of marriage discussed in the sessions. The sessions blend theology and catechesis on the one hand with psychological and pastoral study of skills and practices needed for a healthy marriage on the other. In our own work with couples, John tends to focus on providing more of the theoretical framework (the result of years of university teaching on marriage to undergraduates and seminarians) while Claire focuses more on its practical implementation (the result of her own experience as a wife, mother, and mentor of women and couples). Both of us try to concretize the information with examples drawn from our own life experience, and we encourage the mentor couples using this work to do the same. Mentor couples can decide whether they find it most helpful to read through the catechetical reflections at the beginning of a session with the engaged couples (perhaps taking turns in reading the text), summarizing the main ideas of the material if they are comfortable doing so, or presuming that all present have read the material and moving directly to the discussion questions.

The Background and Title of This Book

This book is the fruit of our own work and experience in the field of marriage ministry in a variety of contexts—academic and pastoral, parish and diocesan, national and international. Over the years, we have both been trained in and taught in a variety of programs—inventory-based, sponsor couple, and diocesan and parish classes. What we have done here is to try to take the strengths of these various programs and blend them with our own study, our experience of some 25 years of intensive work in pre- and post-Cana marriage ministries, as well as our own experience of marriage, to create a new program. While we make no claim that our program is perfect, we do believe that it responds to many of the needs of the Church in the New Evangelization.

The meaning of the book's subtitle ("A Program of Marriage Preparation and Enrichment for the New Evangelization") should now be clear. But what of the title itself?

The phrase "and the two shall become one body" is a translation of Genesis 2:24. The Hebrew word *basar* can either be translated into English as "body" or "flesh." Since the Greek word *sarx* ("flesh") is used when repeating this verse in Ephesians 5:31 (as opposed to *soma,* which means "body"), the latter translation is more common in English versions of the Bible. But there are reasons to prefer the word "body" here beyond personal preference (or the fact that we used it on the cover of our wedding program some thirty-two years ago!).

Throughout the Bible, the body is the basis of all human relationships—with the world, with other human beings, and with God. It is at the heart of the human capacity to give oneself in love—whether in a marriage, priesthood, or consecrated religious life. This is a central idea in Saint John Paul II's magnificent catecheses known as the "Theology of the Body" on which this program draws. Our bodies joined to Christ in Baptism become temples of the Holy Spirit and have an eternal destiny in the resurrection (see 1 Cor 6:13–14, 19). Baptism also makes us members of Christ's body and, hence, members of one another (see 1 Cor 6:15). This image of the Body of Christ is one of Saint Paul's favorite ways to describe the reality of the Church (see 1 Cor 12: 12–26). A Christian marriage is the body of Christ in miniature—a domestic church. In it, Christ lives and acts as priest, prophet, and king. In loving one's spouse and caring for him or her, one loves Christ himself. In their interdependence, spouses learn and live what it means to be "members of one another."

This reality of "becoming one body" is both a gift given to couples on their wedding day when Christ joins them as one, and a task for them to realize over the course of their life together. The letter to the Ephesians speaks of this ongoing task when it tells husbands to love their "wives as their own bodies" (Eph 5:28).[6] The title of this book serves to remind us that for Christians this joining of two bodies, two persons, two lives, takes place within and is sustained by the Body of Christ.

Urbana, MD
December 30, 2017
Feast of the Holy Family

---

[6] All biblical citations in this book are taken from the NABRE.

1

FIRST SESSION

Solitude, Vocation, the Call to Unity

OPENING

SCRIPTURE READING:

GENESIS 2:18–25

SUGGESTED PRAYER[1]:

Lord, You said "it is not good for the man to be alone" and so created the vocation of marriage to answer the longing of our hearts for the communion with each other. Open our minds and hearts to understand Your vision for this vocation more deeply. Bless our time and sharing together with charity toward one another and gratitude for the great gift of marriage. We ask this through Christ our Lord.

---

[1] These suggested opening prayers can be read by a session leader or a volunteer from the group or they can be replaced by another suitable prayer.

CATECHETICAL REFLECTION

On assuming the Chair of Peter, Pope Saint John Paul II chose to devote his weekly general audiences for some five years (1979–1984) to a catechesis on the human person, the body, and sexuality that has come to be known as the "Theology of the Body." Almost every Wednesday (except when he was recovering from an attempted assassination in 1981), he gave an address to a gathering of pilgrims either in Saint Peter's Square or in an audience hall. In these talks, he provided the universal Church with a very profound understanding of the human person as a gift, the human vocation to love, and the way in which this can be realized in the states of marriage or religious celibacy. Because the Church understands Scripture to be "the words of God, expressed in the words of men,"[2] Saint John Paul II turned to Scripture to unpack this understanding of the human person.

Following the lead of Jesus in the Gospels when questioned by the Pharisees about divorce (see Mt 19:3–9), John Paul II returned to the opening chapters of Genesis, especially the second story of creation (Gen 2:4–3:24). Although these texts from Genesis use theological and poetic language, the late Holy Father taught that they comprise our "revealed theological prehistory," which can shed light on our own present-day life and experience.[3] By pondering them, we can come to understand ourselves and the world around us more deeply. He invited us to prayerfully enter into these texts and allow them to shape our understanding of ourselves and our existence.

Created in the state of innocence, the first man discovers his uniqueness compared to the creatures of the world around him through his body.

---

[2] Pope Paul VI, Dogmatic Constitution on Divine Revelation *Dei verbum* (November 18, 1965), §13.

[3] Pope St. John Paul II, *Man and Woman He Created Them: A Theology of the Body*, trans. Michael Waldstein (Boston: Pauline, 2006), no. 4:2 (September 26, 1979), p. 143. All references to the Theology of the Body will be to this edition and will indicate both audience and section number and the page number. The catecheses are also available in a slightly different translation on the Vatican website and can be searched by date.

The animals are created by God (see Gen 2:19–20) and are living things with value, goodness, and purpose; yet they are different from the man. Unlike them, he is aware of himself as a "self" and can freely choose to do or not do certain things. That is to say, he is a person. The other creatures of the world are living things with bodies, but they cannot think, deliberate, and act as he can. Through this encounter with creation, the man becomes aware that his existence is unique—a gift from God. In recognition of this gift he realizes that he is called to return to his Creator in gratitude and obedience. That is, he realizes he is called into a covenant relationship with God. God's command to him defines the terms of this relationship and the limits of his freedom: "You are free to eat from any of the trees of the garden except the tree of knowledge of good and evil. From that tree you shall not eat; when you eat from it you shall die" (Gen 2:16–17). He is therefore called to be *partner of the Absolute* in his capacity to discern between good and evil. The exercise of this capacity in free and deliberate action has the power to bring him life or death.[4]

But even within the unsullied beauty of this new creation, the second story of creation sounds a note of disquiet: "It is not good for the man to be alone" (Gen 2:18). The human person, created for communion with others, discovers a longing in his heart for other human persons with whom he can share his existence and to whom he can give himself in love. For all of us—men and women—solitude can be a gift to discover more deeply our relationship with our Creator, but it can also be a burden that produces loneliness.

God's answer to this dilemma posed by the original solitude of man is to cast the deep sleep on him (the same sleep that precedes Abram's covenant with God in Genesis 15) and to create woman. The man's reaction is a poem of joy which anticipates the later exultation of the Song of Songs: "This one, at last, is bone of my bones and flesh of my flesh; This one shall be called 'woman,' for out of man this one has been taken" (Gen 2:23). He rejoices, Saint John Paul II observes, because he has encountered another body which expresses the person—a body at once like his

---

[4] Ibid., no. 6:2 (October 24, 1979), p. 151. Emphasis original.

own and yet wonderfully different. She is a unique and complimentary way of being a person, a "second 'I.'"[5] In encountering her femininity, he discovers the meaning of his masculinity, and vice versa. The discovery of the opposite sex brings with it *a new consciousness of the meaning of one's* [own] *body.*[6] Yet these sexual differences are themselves the basis for the two being drawn together in attraction and in mutual love. In their movement to "original unity," man and woman become fully the image of God who is Himself an eternal communion of Persons. The full expression of this unity is conveyed through the bodily gift of themselves to one another: "The man and his wife were both naked, yet they felt no shame" (Gen 2:25).[7]

Pope John Paul II's reflections on the text of Genesis help us to see more clearly the dignity of the human person, the importance of the body, and the deep longings of the human heart. In essence, the person is a gift who discovers his or her purpose by learning to give him- or herself to others in love. Saint John Paul II frequently recalled the teaching of the Second Vatican Council in this regard: "man, who is the only creature on earth which God willed for itself, cannot fully find himself except through a sincere gift of himself."[8]

This understanding of the person as gift underlies the Church's vision of the vocation of the human person. Every person discovers the meaning and purpose of his or her humanity in love: "God who created man out of love also calls him to love—the fundamental and innate vocation of every human being" (CCC 1604). The term "vocation" comes from the Latin word *vocare* (to call). So the understanding of the Church is that God has called the human person to fulfill the meaning of his or her existence through learning to receive and give love. And given that the body is the means through which the person discovers and gives him- or herself, the body is an integral part of this vocation. The central role of the body in

---

[5] Ibid., no. 8:4 (November 7, 1979), p. 161.
[6] Ibid., no. 9:5 (November 14, 1979), p. 165.
[7] The full meaning of this "original nakedness" and its relation to the covenant of marriage will be explored in chapter 5.
[8] Second Vatican Council, Pastoral Constitution on the Church in the Modern World *Gaudium et spes* (December 7, 1965), §24 (hereafter cited in the text as GS).

the person's capacity to give and receive love is at the heart of what Pope John Paul II called "the spousal meaning of the body."[9]

In the two fundamental states of Christian life—marriage and religious celibacy—the body plays an integral role. Both are means to give oneself in love to others through one's body. Religious celibates, no less than the married, give the whole of who they are, including their sexuality as men and women, in living out their callings. Married couples give themselves in chaste and faithful love to each other. Celibates give themselves as men and women who practice continence (i.e., refraining from sex) while giving themselves in love to God and in friendship to others in the Body of Christ. Celibacy can even be understood in marital terms as a response to *"Christ the Bridegroom of souls."*[10]

While we often think of vocations in the Church as referring only to the calling to priesthood or religious life, the Church also sees marriage as a vocation: "the vocation to marriage is written in the very nature of man and woman as they came from the hand of the Creator" (CCC 1603). It is a fundamental way for men and women to fulfill their Creator's plan for them by learning to live in love with others. For Christians it is also a way to live out their call to holiness. Through their mutual love they share in and witness to the love of Christ and the Church. The second century Christian writer Tertullian captures something of the beauty of this vocation and the role of the body within it in a treatise written to his wife:

> How can I ever express the happiness of marriage joined by the Church, strengthened by an offering, sealed by a blessing, announced by angels, and ratified by the Father? . . . How wonderful the bond between two believers, now one in hope, one in desire, one in discipline, one in the same service! They are both

---

[9] This term was first used by Pope John Paul II in his weekly general audience of January 2, 1980 (see *Man and Woman He Created Them*, no. 13:1, p. 178) and was used some 117 times in the catecheses. Michael Waldstein calls it "the single most central and important concept in TOB" (ibid., 682).

[10] *Man and Woman He Created Them*, no. 80:1 (April 28, 1982), p. 437. Emphasis original.

children of one Father and servants of the same Master, undivided in spirit and flesh, truly two in one flesh. Where the flesh is one, one also is the spirit.[11]

In learning to live with and for each other and sharing the whole of their lives together, couples learn to give and receive the love that comes from God.

---

[11] Tertullian, *Ad uxorem* (*To My Wife*) 2, 8, 6–7. Cited in the *Catechism of the Catholic Church* 1642 (hereafter CCC).

THOUGHTS FROM CLAIRE: HOW WE MET

I am the youngest and only girl out of four children. I was very close to my mother and spent a lot of time with her. I can remember from a very early age knowing that when I grew up, I wanted to be a wife and mother just like her. I was graced to come to know God's love for me when I was still in grade school and as my relationship with the Lord grew, the Holy Spirit continued to guide me toward my vocation as a married woman. I knew in my heart that this was God's plan for me.

After graduating from a Christian high school on Long Island, I began college at the College of Steubenville in Ohio (now Franciscan University of Steubenville). Although I had been to many youth conferences there and knew that this was where I was meant to be, I never expected that this was where I would meet my future husband and begin my life journey with him.

As a senior in high school, I attended a "come and see" weekend at Steubenville. On the first day while waiting for an elevator I met a nice young man from Puerto Rico named Luis who introduced me to another visiting student named John. John was a high school senior from Milwaukee who was also planning to begin college in the fall.

John and I became friends immediately and spent most of the weekend together. We had a lot of fun attending activities and sharing about our lives back at home. On Sunday we said goodbye, not even exchanging phone numbers or addresses, not knowing (but hoping) that we would meet again.

We both ended up coming to college that fall and during orientation weekend we began running into each other at meetings. It was so nice to see a familiar face, especially after a teary goodbye to my parents. This was the beginning of a very long friendship. After a while, we began to date during our freshman year. John was becoming my best friend, and together we were both growing closer to the Lord; as the years went by we began to discern His plan for our relationship. By the end of our junior year we were sure that we would be married. Two weeks before our graduation in 1985, we got married in my home parish on Long Island and were able to celebrate with family and friends and many of those who shared those four years with us in Steubenville. I still thank God for our wonderful "angel," Luis, who introduced us outside the elevator and whom we never saw again after that weekend.

Discussion Questions:

1. Describe a time when you experienced solitude (an awareness of yourself as a person called by God) as a gift.

2. Why is prayer an inseparable part of the Christian life (CCC 2745)?

3. In what ways do you see your gender (masculinity or femininity) as a gift from God and an integral part of who you are?

4. Describe a time when you experienced solitude as a burden (loneliness or longing for another person).

5. What does every adult have the right and duty to freely choose according to the Church (CCC 2230)?

6. What does consecrated (or religious) life enable a baptized Christian to achieve (CCC 916)?

7. What does the witness of those in consecrated life communicate to the Church and to the world (CCC 933)?

8. When/how did you first become aware that your vocation was to marriage?

9. In the Church's understanding, who is called to holiness (CCC 2013–14)?

10. What sacraments are the foundation of the Christian's vocation to holiness (CCC 1533)?

11. [Couple sharing session only:] Take turns telling the story of how you met. What stands out to you in listening to your fiancée's or spouse's version of your story?

12. When did you first know that your fiancée/spouse was the one whom you were going to marry?

✠ Concluding Prayer ✠

Notes

2

Study Texts

GENESIS 1:26–28

26 Then God said: Let us make human beings in our image, after our likeness. Let them have dominion over the fish of the sea, the birds of the air, the tame animals, all the wild animals, and all the creatures that crawl on the earth.

27 God created mankind in his image;
in the image of God he created them;
male and female he created them.

28 God blessed them and God said to them: Be fertile and multiply; fill the earth and subdue it. Have dominion over the fish of the sea, the birds of the air, and all the living things that crawl on the earth.

GENESIS 2:18–25

18 The LORD God said: It is not good for the man to be alone. I will make a helper suited to him.

19 So the LORD God formed out of the ground all the wild animals and all the birds of the air, and he brought them to the man to see what he would call them; whatever the man called each living creature was then its name.

20 The man gave names to all the tame animals, all the birds of the air, and all the wild animals; but none proved to be a helper suited to the man.

21 So the LORD God cast a deep sleep on the man, and while he was asleep, he took out one of his ribs and closed up its place with flesh.

22 The LORD God then built the rib that he had taken from the man into a woman. When he brought her to the man,

23 the man said:

> "This one, at last, is bone of my bones
> and flesh of my flesh;
> This one shall be called 'woman,'
> for out of man this one has been taken."

24 That is why a man leaves his father and mother and clings to his wife, and the two of them become one body.

25 The man and his wife were both naked, yet they felt no shame.

REFLECTION

The opening chapters of Genesis are foundational for Jews and Christians. They give us a basic understanding of God, the world, ourselves, and the nature of our relationship to Him. The creation of human beings, male and female, is central to these chapters.

In the first, or Priestly, story of creation the account is structured in seven days, indicating the wisdom with which God stills the forces of primeval chaos and shapes the universe. In the first three days, He separates the various elements of the universe—light and darkness, earth and sky, land and sea. Over the next three days, He decorates the world He has made with heavenly luminaries, vegetation, fish and birds, animals, and finally, human beings. The importance of this last event is underscored by the text itself. For the first time, God deliberates over what He is about to do, taking counsel with Himself: "let us make human beings in our image, after our likeness" (1:26).

The Hebrew word for "image" (*selem*) does not imply a physical resemblance to God, but rather that human beings share in God's authority over creation. They exercise dominion over the rest of creation over which they have been placed as stewards. In the words of the second story of creation, they are placed in the world to "cultivate and care for it" (Gen 2:15). At the same time, they have the unique capacity to act as priests for the rest of creation, offering its praise to the One who made it.[1] This role of priest-stewards bespeaks the unique and inalienable dignity of human persons made in the image and likeness of God. As Saint Catherine of Siena exclaims in one of her dialogues with God: "What made you establish man in so great a dignity? Certainly the incalculable love by which you have looked on your creature in yourself! You are taken with love for her; for by love you have created her, by love you have given her a being capable of tasting your eternal Good."[2]

The next verse (Gen 1:27), in a stunning declaration for the time in which it was written, makes clear that this unique dignity and the vocation to act as priest-stewards applies to women as well as men. In fact, it is only in the duality of both sexes—"male and female"—that the image of God is complete in humanity. In their relation to one another, their communion, they fulfill the role God designed for them in creation. For example, one way in which men and women act as stewards and exercise dominion in creation is through their union in marriage, which allows them to share in God's capacity to generate human life: "be fertile and multiply; fill the earth and subdue it" (Gen 1:28). The fruitful union of male and female is the basis of the community of the family and of human society as a whole.

But there is a still more fundamental relation at the heart of human life: the relation between humanity and God expressed in worship. Like the beasts, human beings are created on the sixth day. The number six throughout the Bible denotes incompletion and imperfection. Men and women, like the rest of creation, are complete only in the "rest" of the

---

[1] Many places in Scripture speak metaphorically of creation speaking the praises God. For example, Psalm 19:2: "The heavens declare the glory of God; the firmament proclaims the works of his hands."

[2] St. Catherine of Siena, *Dialogue* 4, 13 "On Divine Providence": *LH*, Sunday, week 19, OR; as cited in CCC 356.

seventh day—a day devoted to the worship of God in ancient Israel. The number seven in biblical literature symbolizes perfection and wholeness, often being associated with God Himself. When men and women worship their Creator, their relationship to creation and to one another is in right order. When they fail to do so, they revert to their origin and become "bestial" in their thought and action.[3] This failure, known in biblical tradition as sin, is the reason why the image of God in humanity was re-drawn and renewed by Christ, the definitive image of God (see Col 1:15–20).

While the first story of creation describes the creation of male and female in God's image simultaneously, the second or Yahwist account separates the creation of woman from man, making it a problem which is resolved by the action of God in the narrative. God fashions man (*adam*) from the clay of the ground (*adamah*) and breathes the breath of life into his nostrils (Gen 2:7). But in stark contrast to the refrain echoing through the first account in which God saw everything that he had made to be "good" (e.g., Gen 1:25) or "very good" (Gen 1:31), the text sounds a strikingly discordant note: "it is *not good* for the man to be alone" (Gen 2:18—emphasis added). God's proposed solution to the problem is to create "a helper suited to him." While in modern English the term "helper" might carry connotations of being secondary or subordinate to someone else, in ancient Hebrew the word *ezer* did not.[4] Woman is created as an equal partner to the man and "helps" him achieve his vocation and mission in the world.

Like man, woman is made directly by God, and like him she is made for God. Her dignity far surpasses that of the animals, none of whom prove to be the "helper suited" to the man (Gen 2:19–20). Instead she is drawn from the side of the man. Saint Thomas Aquinas comments on the

---

[3] In Daniel 4:25–34 King Nebuchadnezzar of Babylon even became beastlike in his appearance after arrogantly failing to acknowledge that all of his power and might came from God. So for a period of seven years he lived with the beasts until his senses were restored to him and he worshipped and acknowledged God as the source of all that he had.

[4] In fact, the term is often applied to God Himself who is the "Help" of Israel. See, for example, Exodus 18:4; Deuteronomy 33:7, 29; and Psalm 20:3; 121:2; 124:8.

fittingness of this: "First, to signify the social union of man and woman, for the woman should neither 'use authority over man,' and so she was not made from his head; nor was it right for her to be subject to man's contempt as his slave, and so she was not made from his feet."[5] Upon seeing her, the man recognizes himself in a new way, declaring "this one shall be called woman [*isha*] for out of man [*ish*] this one has been taken" (Gen 2:23).[6] The point of this play on words is that they are made from the same "stuff" or, more precisely, they possess a common human nature.

In addition to describing their equality in spite of their difference, this text specifies the nature of the unity of man and woman in covenantal language. The nature of a covenant and its relation to this text will be considered more fully in chapter 5. Here we can simply note the concentration of this imagery in Genesis 2:21–25 and its overall effect. The "deep sleep" that God casts on the man in Hebrew is denoted by the Hebrew word *tardemah*—the same term used prior to God's covenant with Abram in Genesis 15:12. God then leads the newly created woman to the man (Gen 2:22), as would the father of the bride in an Israelite wedding ceremony. The man responds with a poem of joy in verse 23, which is also a declaration of his allegiance to her before God. The result of this covenant oath is that the text describes them as "man" and "wife" in Genesis 2:24, highlighting their new unity as "one flesh" with verbs that express covenantal commitment: they "leave" their previous families and "cling" to one another. The covenant of marriage, like the quality and difference of the sexes, is an integral part of God's plan for humanity from the beginning.

---

[5] Thomas Aquinas, *Summa theologica*, trans. Fathers of the English Dominican Province, vol. 2 (New York: Benziger Brothers, 1947) I, q. 92, a. 3. He goes on to point out that it also serves as a symbolic foreshadowing of the Church being born from the pierced side of Christ in the sleep of death on the Cross.

[6] This is the first time in the text that the gender-specific words are used as opposed to the more generic *adam* which can be rendered "man" (in the inclusive sense) or "human."

Questions for Personal Reflection
and Couple Sharing

1. How many times is creation described as "good" or "very good" in Genesis 1:1–2:4? What does this indicate about the physical world around us?

2. How many times does this text use the phrase "God said"? What does this have in common with texts like Exodus 20:1–17? What does this indicate about the connection between creation and God's commands?

3. What is the significance of the seventh day being "holy" or set apart from the others (Gen 2:1–4)?

4. Why is it important to understand human dominion as stewardship over creation and "not as an arbitrary and destructive domination" (CCC 373)?

5. Included in the affirmation of creation as "very good" (Gen 1:31) are sexual differentiation ("male and female") and sexual reproduction ("be fruitful and multiply"). What does this reveal about the goodness of sex as created by God?

6. The Second Vatican Council taught that man (male and female) is "the only creature on earth that God has willed for its own sake" (GS 24). In light of the first story of creation (Gen 1:1–2:4) how would you explain this statement?

7. What does it mean that as the image of God the human being is not just a "something" but a "someone" (CCC 357)?

8. Describe a time or an experience when you came to a deeper appreciation of human dignity (your own or that of someone else).

9. What does it mean that "man and woman are both with one and the same dignity 'in the image of God'" (CCC 369)?

10. What are some of the ways in which men and women are complementary to each other or able to serve as one another's "helpmates" (CCC 372)?

11. What are the two basic ends or purposes of sexual union in marriage in the eyes of the Church (CCC 2363)?

12. How are these purposes intimated in the texts of Genesis (see 1:28 and 2:24–25)?

13. The Second Vatican Council also taught that: "In reality it is only in the mystery of the Word made flesh that the mystery of man truly becomes clear. . . . Christ, the final Adam, by the mystery of the revelation of the Father and his love, fully reveals man to man himself and makes his supreme calling clear" (GS, §22). How does Christ complete our understanding of what it means to be the image of God?

14. How does Christ deepen our understanding of our vocation to be the priest-stewards of the created world?

Notes

3

SECOND SESSION
"To Leave and to Cling": Forming a New Family

OPENING

SCRIPTURE READINGS:
GENESIS 2:24; MATTHEW 19:4

SUGGESTED PRAYER:
Lord, You willed that man and wife be joined together into one body. Thank You for the covenant and Sacrament of Marriage that creates this domestic church. Deepen our communion of love as couples and help it to bear fruit in the community of our families, the Church, and the world.

CATECHETICAL REFLECTION

Read in its historical context, the text of Genesis 2:24 is striking for its reversal of the law and practice of marriage in ancient Israel. The narrator intones, "That is why a man leaves his father and mother and clings to his wife, and the two of them become one body."

Much of the second story of creation (i.e., Genesis 2:4–3:24) has an etiological character. That is, it seeks to offer an explanation of how things got to be the way they are. In this it resembles much of the Wisdom literature of the Old Testament. This is especially true of the account of the Fall of man and woman in chapter 3 which offers an explanation for, among other things, shame, the disordering of sexual desire, the human fear of serpents, the conflict between the sexes, pain in childbirth, toil in work, and the reality of death as part of life in a fallen world.

But here at the end of chapter 2 we have what seems to be an explanation for the practice of marriage. However, on closer examination, this verse does not describe the practice of marriage in Ancient Israelite law; in many ways, it reverses it. Men did not leave their families to marry their wives; it was women who left their families to become part of the family of a man. Unlike modern Judaism, which is matriarchal, in ancient Israel family lineage was patriarchal—that is, it was traced through the male line. Hence upon marriage, a woman became part of the house of her husband. In the New Testament Jesus is described as being of the House of David because Joseph was of the line of David—even though Joseph was only his foster father (see Mt 1:1–17).

Saint John Paul II in his Theology of the Body catecheses sees Genesis 2:24 as an identification of the essential properties of marriage as understood in the Catholic Tradition. Commenting on Jesus' invocation of it in His response to the Pharisees' question concerning divorce, he notes that Jesus underscores the weighty character of the verse adding the declaration: "So they are no longer two, but one flesh. Therefore what God has joined let not man separate" (Mt 19:6). Saint John Paul II writes, "That phrase, 'let not man separate' is decisive. In the light of the word of Christ, Genesis 2:24 states the principle of the unity and indissolubility of marriage as the very content of the word of God expressed in the most ancient revelation."[1] So through marriage man and woman form together a new entity which Genesis describes in the language of "one flesh."[2] This union has an unbreakable character which Saint John Paul II, following

---

[1] *Man and Woman He Created Them*, no. 1:3 (September 5, 1979), p. 132. See also 2.2 (September 12, 1979), p. 134.

[2] As noted in the introduction to this book, the Hebrew word *basar* can be translated into English as either "body" or "flesh."

the Catholic Tradition, calls "indissoluble." It is important to see that this is not a legal requirement of marriage created by the Church. Our Lord Himself affirms and clarifies that it was God's plan for marriage from creation.

While later Old Testament law would allow for divorce—particularly of women by their husbands (see Deut 24:1–4)—Jesus insists that this was a concession to human hard-heartedness (see Mt 19:8). Many rabbis in Jesus' time held the view that some provisions of the Law were temporary measures for a fallen world which would be lifted when the messiah came. Jesus confirms this to be the case, and, by His own authority as the promised Messiah, He prophetically reinstates God's plan for marriage from creation. But, Jesus is not just the promised Messiah. As Son of God, He is the New Moses who not only reveals more clearly but actually makes possible the living out of God's plan for marriage. We will consider this healing and transformation of marriage by Christ more fully in upcoming chapters.

For now, let us return to the puzzling statement of the narrator in Genesis 2:24 that it is a man who leaves his family to be joined to his wife. Pope Francis notes that the Hebrew word "to cleave" or "to be joined" (*dabaq*) connotes intimacy. The word, he says, "bespeaks a profound harmony, a closeness that is both physical and interior, to such an extent that the word is used to describe our union with God: 'My soul clings to you.' (Ps 63:8)" (AL 13). Some biblical commentators suggest that this reversal of the legal practice of Ancient Israel might show awareness of the need for spouses (and perhaps particularly men) to detach themselves from their family of origin—not just physically, but emotionally—to fully enter into marriage.

It is undoubtedly true that in some way everyone is a "product" of the family by which he or she came into the world. Our parents form us not only by passing on their genes, but in a whole variety of other ways—social, economic, historical, and interpersonal. As Saint John Paul II taught: "When a new person is born of the conjugal union of the two, he brings with him into the world a particular image and likeness of God himself: *the genealogy of the person is inscribed in the very biology of generation*."[3] The family is where a person is socialized through learning basic human (and, for believers, Christian) values. By learning to relate to parents and siblings, children learn values like respect, justice, and compassion. These values enable them to come to see others and the world around them as a gift. As Pope Francis puts it: "In the family we receive an integral education, which enables us to grow harmoniously in personal maturity. In the family we learn to ask without demanding, to say 'thank you' as an expression of genuine gratitude for what we have been given, to control our aggressivity and greed, and to ask forgiveness when we have caused harm. These simple gestures of heartfelt courtesy help to create a culture of shared life and respect for our surroundings."[4] The family through which we come into the world is an integral part of our identity. It thus serves as the "original cell" of human society by forming its future members (CCC 2207).

That is why tragedy, trauma, and loss in the early part of a person's life can create deep and enduring wounds. Whether it be abandonment, the death of a parent or sibling, a family fractured by divorce, or growing up in situations of war or poverty, such life-altering events can have a lasting effect on people, coloring their perception of the world with fear and loss and making it more difficult for them to enter into deep and lasting friendships such as marriage. Sometimes lasting wounds can have less dramatic causes—a distant or unloving parent, a difficult relationship with a sibling, a family forced to move frequently by work, economic conditions, or military service. When there are significant issues in someone's personality or relationships, professional counseling before or (if they surface later) during marriage can be a wise choice (see AL 236, 239–40).

But everyone brings things from their childhood experience and upbringing into a marriage: habits, traditions, expectations and assumptions about how marriage and family life should work. Some of these may

---

[3] Pope St. John Paul II, Letter to Families *Gratissimam sane* (February 2, 1994), §9. Emphasis original.

[4] Pope Francis, Encyclical Letter on Care for Our Common Home *Laudato si'* (May 24, 2015), §213.

be good (such as prioritizing one's faith or time spent together), some may be bad (such as destructive ways of resolving conflict or being taught to never express emotions), and some may be neutral (such as assumptions about how holidays should be celebrated or which spouse should be responsible for certain household tasks). One could imagine all of these habits, traditions, expectations, and assumptions as "baggage" that a couple brings into the marriage from their families of origin. One of the tasks of engagement and the early part of marriage is sorting through much of this baggage and deciding together which "bags" a couple wants to keep, which they want to discard, and which they want to modify. In regard to things like traditions, expectations, and assumptions, much of this work can be done through establishing and maintaining good communication and conflict resolution patterns in the relationship.

Conflict, when properly handled and resolved, can be a means to continue to surface unspoken expectations and unmet needs, providing a doorway to deeper intimacy in the relationship. The whole of this process of sorting through baggage together is sustained by the grace of the sacrament, enabling working communication, daily reconciliation, and growth in mutual understanding. The fruit of this work by a couple is growth toward the "one flesh" unity of mind, heart, and life with which Scripture describes their relationship.

Thoughts from Claire: Creating Our Own Traditions

Imagine being a new bride, starting a brand new family with the love of your life, and suddenly having your husband's family angry at you simply for doing things differently from them. Not the best way to start out in a marriage. John and I had to learn early on that we needed to set boundaries with our extended families in order to strengthen our own relationship and to protect our new little "domestic church."

Setting boundaries with my own family wasn't too hard, especially since my parents lived on Long Island and John and I had moved to Milwaukee so he could begin graduate school. I realized later that a little distance from family of origin for newly married couples could actually be a very good thing. It turned out that Marquette University was actually in John's hometown, so we ended up living just three miles from his mother. She was older than my parents and had been a widow for some years, used to being in charge and expecting her family to do things her way.

The first couple years of marriage were a bit stressful, especially around the holidays. It was expected that we were going to have all of the same traditions that John's family had. But they were very different from what I was used to. We were even expected to spend every Sunday with my mother-in-law since Sundays were "family day." Needless to say, when I made it known that this just wasn't going to work, I was not very popular with John's family. It took a while, but John and I learned the importance of communicating with each other about our own expectations and what we wanted for our new family. It wasn't until we realized the importance of being one—agreeing on how we were going to spend our time and what traditions we wanted to make our own—that we began to feel peaceful in our marriage and develop a sense of how God wanted to lead us in our new family. We began to pray for God's guidance and wisdom for our family and in our relationships with our extended families. We did realize that the key was asking God for help and making sure that we were a united front—not just with our kids in our home, but with our extended families outside of it.

Once we realized the importance of beginning our own traditions, it was a lot of fun. When the kids were little, we decided that at Christmastime we needed some time to just be a family. Christmas day was always time to spend with the relatives so we decided that Christmas Eve would be our time. John saw that I needed time to relax so he suggested that we make it easy on me by not having me cook that night. This is the origin of our tradition (which we still do with our grown children) of going to Christmas Eve Mass and then out for Chinese food. Even on a tight budget, a meal at a Chinese restaurant was always pretty reasonable. Then we would come home to Christmas cookies and a Christmas movie. In the morning, we would have our special breakfast, pray as family, and then open presents—one at a time, of course—helping us to be grateful for all of the blessings God had given us. The rest of the day was always filled with visiting with friends and extended family.

The next thirty years were filled with many new practices and traditions, some lasting and some not. The important ones are still present in our family—praying together, eating meals together, watching Green Bay Packer games together, and, most importantly, going to Mass together. Even on vacation we always make time for Mass as a family. It is a blessing to see how our new practices and traditions have helped to form our children into faithful Catholics who love the Lord and love life.

Discussion Questions:

1. What are some of the gifts and positive traits which you see in yourself that you bring from your family of origin?

2. What are some of gifts and positive traits which you see in your fiancée/ spouse which are also evident in his or her family of origin?

3. What are some negative patterns or traits in your family of origin which you do not want to carry forward in your family founded by marriage?

4. What are some negative patterns or traits in your fiancée/spouse's family of origin that you do not want to see carried forward in your family?

5. Scripture speaks of the sins of parents being "visited upon" children to the third or fourth generation (see Ex 20:5–6, 34:6–7; Num 14:18; Deut 5:9–10). Social science verifies that cycles of brokenness and dysfunction in families (such as abuse, addiction, violence, or divorce) can replicate themselves across generations. Are there any such issues in your own family tree? What steps have you taken to deal with them?

6. Scripture also speaks of God's blessing being passed on across generations to those who love and serve Him (see Ex 20:6; Deut 7:9; Ps 103:17, 112:2). How have you seen God's gifts or blessings at work across generations in your family?

7. How have you seen God's grace bring healing within the relationships in your family of origin?

8. What relationships in your family of origin are still in need of healing?

9. Among people that you know, who has the strongest marriage? What makes the relationship strong?

10. What holiday traditions in your family of origin do you most value?

11. How would you like to carry forward those traditions in your new family?

12. [Fill in the blank] I think that I should be able to spend _____ dollars without first having to discuss it with my (future) spouse.[5]

13. [Fill in the blank] I think that _____ should be in charge of our finances. Explain.

14. If my spouse gets a job that requires us to move to a different city or state, I will:

15. Guess the date of the birth of your next child:

---

[5] Questions 12–16 are adapted from Robert Ruhnke, CSSR, *The Sponsor Couple for Christian Marriage Preparation: For Better and Forever* (Liguori, MO: Liguori Publications, 1989), evening 2.

16. Surfacing Assumptions about Couple Responsibilities

For each task below indicate whether you think that it should be done by the husband, the wife, or both. Indicate your answer with an "H" for "husband," a "W" for "wife," and a "B" for "both." Be prepared to explain your answers and the assumptions that underlie them.

A. [ ] set the alarm for waking up
B. [ ] make coffee
C. [ ] fix breakfast on weekdays
D. [ ] fix breakfast on weekends
E. [ ] make the bed
F. [ ] shop for food
G. [ ] prepare dinner
H. [ ] clean the kitchen after dinner
I. [ ] get children ready for bed
J. [ ] clean the house
K. [ ] do laundry
L. [ ] take care of the yard
M. [ ] take care of the plants/garden
N. [ ] pay bills
O. [ ] manage shared social media
P. [ ] oversee auto maintenance/repairs
Q. [ ] oversee tech maintenance/repairs
R. [ ] plan weekends
S. [ ] schedule social activities
T. [ ] initiate couple/family prayer
U. [ ] initiate reconciliation after an argument
V. [ ] initiate sex
W. [ ] schedule participation in liturgical worship
X. [ ] pick up my dirty clothes
Y. [ ] shop for birthday and Christmas presents for relatives
Z. [ ] write Christmas cards

✠ Concluding Prayer ✠

Notes

4

Study Texts

JOHN 2:1–11

1 On the third day there was a wedding in Cana in Galilee
and the mother of Jesus was there.

2 Jesus and his disciples were also invited to the wedding.

3 When the wine ran short, the mother of Jesus said to him,
"They have no wine."

4 [And] Jesus said to her,
"Woman, how does your concern affect me?
My hour has not yet come."

5 His mother said to the servers,
"Do whatever he tells you."

6 Now there were six stone water jars there for Jewish
ceremonial washings,
each holding twenty to thirty gallons.

7 Jesus told them, "Fill the jars with water."
So they filled them to the brim.

8 Then he told them,
"Draw some out now and take it to the headwaiter."
So they took it.

9 And when the headwaiter tasted the water that had become wine,
without knowing where it came from

(although the servers who had drawn the water knew),

the headwaiter called the bridegroom

10 and said to him,

"Everyone serves good wine first and then when people have drunk

freely,

an inferior one;

but you have kept the good wine until now."

11 Jesus did this as the beginning of his signs in Cana in Galilee

and so revealed his glory and his disciples began to believe in him.

REFLECTION

Weddings in Jesus' day, as in ours, were important occasions. They were crucial social and religious events celebrated within families. Usually they took place right in the family's home rather than in a religious building like a synagogue or the Temple. To run out of wine, as happened at the celebration in this text, would have been a major embarrassment for the host family and for the groom. On one level, it appears that Jesus' first miracle described in John's Gospel is an act of kindness, performed at the prompting of His mother, to avert such a social faux pas in front of the family and friends of the couple.

But if we pay careful attention to the language and imagery of the passage, especially in light of the rest of John's Gospel and the Bible as a whole, it is clear that there is much more going on in this text.

Wine is a natural symbol of joy and fulfillment—hence its role in a celebration such as a wedding. To run out indicates a crisis deeper than social embarrassment. It speaks of the failure of human resources to sustain the happiness for which we hunger.

Mary is sensitive to this potential crisis and intercedes with her Son to avert it. Jesus' use of the term "woman" foreshadows His use of this same form of address to her from the Cross (see Jn 19:26). It also recalls the "woman" of the opening chapters of Genesis. While that woman (Eve) played an integral role in the Fall of humanity into sin, Mary, the New

40

Eve, encourages faith and obedience to the New Adam (Jesus), telling the servants to "do whatever he tells you." Later when she is addressed by the same term from the Cross ("Woman, behold your son"), she will be entrusted with the care of the Beloved Disciple, who is the model of believing readers of the Gospel. This suggests her maternal role in the lives of Christians. In her care for us, Mary points us to Christ.

The six stone jars are also significant. As noted in the first chapter, the number 6 is used throughout the Bible as a symbol of incompletion and imperfection. That is because it is one short of seven, the number of perfection. So, in Genesis, human beings are created with the beasts on the sixth day, but only complete in the sabbath worship of the seventh (see Gen 1:26–2:4). The Beast of Revelation, who sets itself up in God's place (see Rev 13:15–18), is designated as a kind of unholy trinity with the number 666. Here it is stone jars used "for Jewish ceremonial washing" that are given this symbolic number of incompleteness. In this designation John's Gospel has in mind the law and ritual worship of the Old Testament, which are lacking in power to transform those who participate in it. Among these rituals, the setting of the passage reminds us, is marriage itself. Marriage, though good and created by God, falls short in the face of human limitation and sin—it needs something more.

In spite of His seemingly brusque response to His mother, Jesus acts in response to her plea. The ritual and law of the Old Covenant which lacked the power to cleanse is replaced by the new wine which Jesus gives—a wine of surpassing excellence. The wedding celebration is transformed by this action of Jesus. The result, the Gospel tells us, is that "he revealed his glory" and his disciples "began to believe in him" (see v. 11).

This sign that Jesus works, like all of the signs in the Fourth Gospel, points to and reflects His "hour" (see v. 4). This term, when it is used in the Fourth Gospel, refers to the "hour" of His glorification in the Cross, Resurrection, and Ascension (see John 13:1). This is where Jesus' glory is fully revealed—the same glory He had with the Father before the world began (see John 1:14). Jesus' miraculous action at this wedding anticipates and makes present His transformation of the world by His being "lifted up" for us (see John 12:32).

When we consider this event in the light of the whole of the Bible, we realize that the setting of a wedding celebration is not an accident. Later in the Gospel, John the Baptist will describe Jesus in His mission as "the bridegroom" and himself as the "best man" who attends Him (Jn 3:29–30). Old Testament prophets such as Hosea, Jeremiah, and Ezekiel used this same image to describe Yahweh as the Bridegroom in His covenant relationship with the people of Israel. John's use of this image to describe Jesus points to His divine origin with the Father, which He depicted in the opening verses of his Gospel (see John 1:1–3). The Letter to the Ephesians will describe Christian marriage as a "great mystery" which reflects the union between Christ the Bridegroom and the Church, His Bride (see Eph 5:21–32). The Book of Revelation describes heaven as the celebration of the "wedding feast of the Lamb" (Rev 19:7–9). The mystery of God's relationship to His people in both the Old Covenant and the New is marital. Marriage discloses the nature of who God is and how He loves us. This saving love is revealed in a new and transformative way in Christ. The "new wine" of marriage in Christ is surpassingly better than marriage as a natural, created reality.

Saint John Chrysostom, the great preacher of the fourth-century Eastern Church, used the text of Cana to exhort couples to invite Christ to their wedding so that He could likewise transform their marriages: "If you drive away the other things, Christ himself will come to your wedding, and where Christ goes the angels' choir follows. If you ask Him, He will work an even greater miracle than he worked in Cana: that is, He will transform the water of your unstable passions into the wine of spiritual unity."[1] For Saint John and for other Fathers of the Church, Cana points to the reality of Jesus' presence and action in the celebration of Christian marriage. This is not just a story about something that happened at the beginning of Jesus' public ministry. It is a description of His ongoing role in uniting His followers, transforming their love for each other into a reflection and a participation in His own love.

---

[1]   St. John Chrysostom, *Homily 12 on Colossians* [on Col 4:18]. Cited in *On Marriage and Family Life*, trans. Catherine Roth and David Anderson, ed. Catherine Roth (Crestwood, NY: Saint Vladimir's, 1986), 78.

As John's Gospel itself indicates, this love is reflected most clearly in Christ's sacrificial gift of Himself on the Cross. Saint Thomas Aquinas teaches that all of "the sacraments of the Church derive their power specially from Christ's Passion."[2] Marriage is unique among the sacraments in that it is conformed to the Passion through the intensity of Jesus' love, "whereby He suffered for the Church who was to be united to Him as His spouse."[3]

This life-giving gift of Himself in love is precisely what we receive when we eat the Body and Blood of Christ in the Eucharist (see John 6:51–58) which is itself a foretaste of the eternal Wedding Feast of the Lamb. Commenting on the text of Cana Pope Benedict XVI offers a beautiful synthesis of these aspects of the mystery of salvation present within it:

[Jesus] gives a sign which proclaims his hour, the hour of the wedding feast, the hour of union between God and man. He does not merely "make" wine but transforms the human wedding feast into an image of the divine wedding feast, to which the Father invites us through the Son and in which he gives every good thing, represented by the abundance of wine. The wedding feast becomes an image of that moment when Jesus pushed love to the utmost, let his body be rent and gave himself to us forever, having become completely one with us—a marriage between God and man. The hour of the cross, the hour which is the source of the sacrament, in which he gives himself really to us in flesh and blood, puts his body into our hands and our hearts; this is the hour of the wedding feast. . . . Jesus' hour is the cross; his definitive hour will be his return at the end of time.[4]

---

[2] *Summa theologica* III, q. 62, a. 5.

[3] Ibid., Supplement, q. 42, a. 1, ad. 3. Cited in Fathers of the English Dominican Province, *Summa theologica*, vol. 3, 2715.

[4] Pope Benedict XVI, "Homily of the Holy Father," Altötting, Germany, September 11, 2006, https://w2.vatican.va/content/benedict-xvi/en/homilies/2006/documents/hf_ben-xvi_hom_20060911_shrine-altotting.html.

One concrete implication of this is that the Eucharist is central to the spiritual life of a couple and their family: "For the food of the Eucharist offers the spouses the strength and incentive needed to live the marriage covenant each day as a 'domestic church'" (AL 316).

Marriage is thus an integral part of how God reveals Himself to us and unites us to Himself. It is not just a holy sign. It is a sacrament—a sign which communicates His transforming grace and life to us who receive it. Cana, along with other biblical texts, enables us to begin to see this mystery.

Questions for Personal Reflection and Couple Sharing

1. Compare the words and actions of Mary in John 2:3–5 with those of Eve in Genesis 3:1–6. What qualities do each of them show?

2. How have you experienced Mary inviting you to a deeper relationship with Jesus in your own life?

3. Saint Thomas Aquinas teaches that the Mother of Jesus is present at every Christian wedding. How did/will your own wedding celebration reflect this reality?

4. There are numerous parallels between the account of Cana in John 2 and the Passion of Jesus in John 19. Note the similarities and differences in the use of the following ideas:

John 2:1–11	**John 19:16–30**
"the mother of Jesus" (2:1)	"his mother" (19:25)
"woman" (2:4)	"woman" (19:26)
"no wine" (2:3)	"common wine" (19:29)
"my hour" (2:4)	"from that hour" (19:27)
"six stone jars" (2:6)	"a vessel" (19:29)
"water" (2:7)	"blood and water" (19:34)
"and so revealed his glory" (2:11)	"An eyewitness has testified and his testimony is true" (19:35)
"and his disciples began to believe in him" (2:11)	"so that you may come to believe" (19:35)

5. What do these parallels suggest about the nature of God's love for us revealed in the Passion of Christ?

6. What do these parallels suggest about the nature of love within Christian marriage (see Eph 2:25–27)?

7. What is the highest demonstration of love according to these New Testament passages?

- John 3:16 —

- Romans 5:8 —

- 1 John 4:10 —

8. Compare Matthew 19:3–9 to Deuteronomy 24:1–4. What change did Jesus make in regard to marriage?

9. How do you hope that Christ will transform your relationship with your fiancée (or spouse) in your marriage?

10. Saint John Chrysostom told the Christians of his day that they could invite Christ to their weddings by inviting members of the clergy or the poor to their celebrations. Name three things couples planning a wedding today could do to invite Christ to be present.

11. Based on your study of John 2:1–11, why do you think that the Church recommends that marriage be celebrated in the context of the Eucharist whenever possible?

12. Why is it important to strive for simplicity in the wedding celebration of a Christian couple?

Notes

5

THIRD SESSION
Marriage as a Covenant and a Sacrament

OPENING

SCRIPTURE READING:
JOHN 2:1–11

SUGGESTED PRAYER:

Lord Jesus, You revealed Your glory in the sign You worked at the wedding feast of Cana. We ask You to be present in our lives and relationships and to transform our love for each other so that it is a sharing in Your own unconditional love for us. Let our marriages overflow with the new and abundant wine of the Holy Spirit so that they can reflect Your glory to the world around us. We ask this in Your name. Amen.

CATECHETICAL REFLECTION

As should be clear from the previous chapters, in the Scriptures marriage is described as a covenant. Texts like Proverbs 2:17 and Malachi 2:14 use the actual Hebrew word for covenant (*berit*) to designate the marital relationship. Other texts such as Genesis 2:21–25 do not use the word itself but are full of language and images that describe the relationship of man and woman in covenantal terms. One way to understand the nature of such a covenant is to contrast it with a contract.

A contract in the Bible is understood as a legal agreement between two parties based on a promise of property. Two individuals (usually men) would go to the elders at the gate of their city or town (the ancient Israelite equivalent of a courtroom) and describe the agreement they were making with each other. In making the promise, they would also specify property that they would surrender if they failed to keep the terms of their contract (e.g., a certain number of livestock of equivalent value). Because this contract was witnessed by other Israelites, it was considered legally binding on those who made it. If one of them broke the agreement, he would then surrender the property to the other.

A covenant is different from this in a number of ways. In a covenant the two parties did not swear merely before human witnesses; they swore an oath of fidelity before God. Even if God was one of the parties of the covenant (as in the covenant between Yahweh and Israel), this was the case because there was nothing higher on which to swear. Furthermore, the parties in a covenant did not offer specific possessions as the pledge for keeping their word—instead they swore on their own lives.

This reality is vividly described in Genesis 15. Abram (not yet renamed Abraham) makes a covenant with Yahweh. God has Abram sacrifice animals and cut the larger ones in two halves. Typically, in such a ceremony both parties would walk between the sacrificed animals, signifying by that act that if they ever broke their pact, their own lives would be similarly forfeit. The fact that only God does so in this case (in the form of a smoking brazier and torch) indicates that this is a unilateral covenant—God promises to be faithful even if Abram and his descendants are not.

A covenant has two basic components: an oath of fidelity sworn to another party (on one's own life) and a sign or gesture that enacts and seals that oath. For example, in Exodus 24 the people of Israel, now freed from their bondage in Egypt, swear an oath to keep the terms of their covenant with the Lord: "We will do everything that the Lord has told us" (Ex 24:3). Moses then seals the covenant by sprinkling blood on both the altar and the people. Because blood is symbolic of life, this gesture expresses the reality that God and the people now share a common life. Other gestures used to seal and express a covenant include sharing meals (a sign of familial intimacy as we saw in the second session), a handshake (still used in our culture in the context of business agreements), or the bestowal of a garment (a symbolic promise of care and responsibility).

In the case of marriage, the oath takes the form of a declaration of fidelity made before God: "This one, at last, is bone of my bones and flesh of my flesh" (Gen 2:23), says the man. As we saw earlier, the language of "bone" and "flesh" is a declaration of allegiance or kinship (2 Sam 5:1). Furthermore, "bone" in the Bible is often used as a symbol of strength or power (Gen 26:16),[1] while "flesh" is a symbol of weakness (Is 40:6–8). So this declaration of the man in binding himself to the women covers the full range of human possibilities as modern wedding vows promise faithfulness "in sickness and in health." The sign or gesture that seals or ratifies this covenant is more cryptically expressed: "The man and his wife were both naked, yet they felt no shame" (Gen 2:25). The bodily intimacy of the couple indicated by their "nakedness" fully expresses their unity and serves as the sign of the first marriage covenant.

Saint John Paul II in his Theology of the Body catecheses repeatedly reminds us that the body is the expression and revelation of the person. The body speaks both in its existence and in its activity. Simply in its masculinity and femininity, the body communicates the reality of the person and the person's ability to give him- or herself in love. This is what the late Pope referred to as "the spousal meaning of the body": "The human body with its sex—its masculinity and femininity—seen in the very mystery of creation, is not only a source of fruitfulness and procreation, as in the whole natural order, but contains 'from the beginning' the 'spousal' attribute, that is, *the power to express love: precisely that love in which the human person becomes a gift* and—through this gift—fulfills

---

[1] While our English translations typically have Abimelech saying to Isaac "you have become too powerful for me," the Hebrew literally says "you are breaking my bones"—hence the association of "bone" and "power."

the very meaning of his being and existence."[2] This capacity to radiate the truth of the person through the body was especially profound in the state of original innocence in which this communication was unhindered by the constraints of competing drives and the personal and interpersonal fragmentation introduced by sin.

In addition to the communication of the person through the body's masculinity or femininity, the body also communicates the person through action. This is an aspect of what the late Pope referred to as "the language of the body." Much of human communication is nonverbal, taking the form of bodily posture, facial expressions, and physical gestures. But John Paul II also understood particular actions or gestures to have an intrinsic meaning to them, given to them by God. In such a case, the body "speaks a language of which it is not the author."[3] In the case of sexual intimacy in marriage, the meaning of this bodily action derives from the covenant promise the couple exchanges in entering marriage. This promise becomes the basis of the whole of their life together, including their sexual relationship:

> The words, "I take you as my wife/as my husband," bear within themselves that perennial and ever unique and unrepeatable "language of the body," and they place it at the same time in the communion of persons. . . . In this way the . . . "language of the body" *is not only the "substratum,"* but *in some sense also the constitutive content of the communion of persons.* The persons—the man and the woman—become a reciprocal gift for each other. They become this gift in their masculinity and femininity while they discover the spousal meaning of the body and refer it reciprocally to themselves in an irreversible way: in the dimension of life as a whole.[4]

---

[2] *Man and Woman He Created Them*, 15:1 (January 16, 1980), pp. 185–86. Emphasis original.

[3] Ibid., 105:6 (January 19, 1983), p. 541.

[4] Ibid., 103:5 (January 5, 1983), p. 533. Emphasis original.

Hence in their wedding vows a man and woman make a gift of themselves to each other. They promise fidelity and the whole of who they are as persons. This mutual gift then becomes the basis of the whole of their life together—their communion of love. This gift is remembered and expressed in a unique way in the bodily language spoken in sexual intercourse.

This is one reason why the prophets of the Old Testament could compare Israel's worship of other gods as a form of adultery or "playing the harlot." As we saw in the previous chapter, the covenant between Israel and God was also marital. It was rooted in promises of total fidelity expressed in the worship of only Yahweh. Under the influence of this great sign at the heart of their lives, the people of Israel came to understand the necessity of fidelity within the covenant of marriage. As Pope Benedict XVI says, "Corresponding to the image of a monotheistic God is monogamous marriage."[5] But the people of Israel also came to realize God's tender and passionate love for them. God is like a husband who passionately pursues and tenderly loves his bride, even when she was not faithful to him. This revelation of God's passionate love for us culminates in Christ the Bridegroom laying down His life for His Bride, the Church. In His act of love, sacrificial self-gift (*agapē*) and passionate desire for union (*eros*) are completely interwoven. This is the intimate love that we receive in the Eucharist.[6] This is the divine love at the heart of Christian marriage.

Christian marriage is a covenant, but it is more than this. It is more than a covenant uniting a man and woman before God. It is more than a sign of God's marital union with His people in the Old and New Covenants. It is also a participation in the union between Christ and the Church that communicates God's transforming life and love. That is, it is a sacrament. Sacraments are efficacious signs. They not only are symbols of holy things; they communicate grace (God's own uncreated life) to us.

Corresponding to the oath of the marriage covenant is the couple's

---

5   Pope Benedict XVI, Encyclical Letter on Christian Love *Deus caritas est* (December 25, 2005), §11.

6   See ibid., §§12–14.

expression of consent in their wedding vows. A couple makes a free and conscious choice to bind themselves to one another in the midst of the Christian community. They promise to be faithful to one another and to love and honor one another for the whole of their lives. In so doing, they make a gift of themselves to each other. This gift includes the whole of who they are as a man and a woman which includes their fertility— their capacity to cooperate with God in bringing children into the world. Therefore, consent is ordered to and expressed in sexual consumma- tion—the sign or gesture that fully enacts this covenant promise.[7] The "language of the body" spoken in marital sex, therefore, is a recollection and an enactment of their vows to each other. This does not mean that every time a couple has intercourse they mystically relive their wedding vows. It means that giving themselves to each other sexually—whether they are tired or energetic, anxious or joyful, aware of its full meaning or not—expresses in a bodily way the promises that united them as husband and wife.

In the understanding of the Western Church, it is the couple them- selves in virtue of their baptism who confer the sacrament on each other. Pope John Paul II says of the exchange of vows: "With these words the engaged couple contract marriage, and at the same time they receive it as a sacrament of which they are both ministers. *Both, the man and the woman, administer the sacrament.* They do so before witnesses. The authorized witness is the priest, who at the same time blesses the mar- riage and presides over the whole liturgy of the sacrament."[8] The priest generally must be there along with other witnesses (usually two), but, in some sense, he is expendable. Christ acts in and through the couple to unite them before the Church community.[9]

---

[7] As John Paul II expresses it, "the words themselves, 'I take you as my wife/my husband' do not only refer to a determinate reality, but they can only be fulfilled by the *copula conjugale* (conjugal intercourse)" (*Man and Woman He Created Them*, 103:2 [January 5, 1983], p. 532). Technically the expression of consent causes the sacrament while sexual consummation makes it indissoluble.

[8] Ibid., 103:1 (January 5, 1983), p. 531.

[9] In the understanding of the Eastern Churches (Catholic and Orthodox) it is the priest who is the minister of the sacrament in conferring the nuptial blessing on the couple. These differences are not as great as they might seem insofar as the

When a couple is joined in marriage, a bond is created that gives them a new identity as husband and wife. This bond becomes an ongoing source of God's grace to sustain and empower the couple over the whole of their life together.[10] It is vital that couples seek to practice and deepen their faith so that they can consciously draw upon the grace of the sacrament in facing the joys and challenges of married life together. Sacramental marriage gives them the power to love, to serve, and to forgive in ways that go beyond the limits of human resources. The new wine of the Holy Spirit far exceeds the water of human effort.

Western Church generally requires a priest for a valid marriage and the Eastern Churches presuppose the consent of the couple (which is sometimes expressed in a betrothal ceremony). All of these Churches understand that it is Christ (whether acting through the couple or the priest) who joins a husband and wife in sacramental marriage.

[10] The Western Church has generally seen this bond dissolved by death ("until death do us part"). Some of the Eastern Churches understand the bond to continue after the death of one or both spouses, but still allow for remarriage after one loses a spouse.

THOUGHTS FROM CLAIRE:
THE GRACE OF THE SACRAMENT

Being called to the covenant of marriage is something that I believed was God's will for me for as long as I can remember. While I knew that I wanted to be a wife and mother ever since I was young, I did not know what a promise of faithful love to another person entailed. Along with the joy and excitement that come when you make a covenant with another person come great suffering and trials as well.

As we saw in our study of the covenant we make when we become husband and wife, the bond that is created between the couple becomes an ongoing source of God's grace in marriage. In the Sacrament of Marriage the grace that God pours out upon us helps us through the good times and bad times, through the joys and the sufferings, and in sickness and in health. This means that we don't have to do this on our own. God's grace, through the Holy Spirit, is there to help us in our life together.

Right from the beginning of our marriage, John and I have had to rely on this grace. In our first year together, we were blessed to conceive our first child, our beautiful daughter Rachel Elizabeth. I must admit that being pregnant was not all that fun for me—or for John. I had morning sickness for almost nine solid months and I am sure that I wasn't easy to live with. By turning to the sacramental grace that God had given us in our marriage, John was able to love me and serve me even through this hard time, and I learned to accept unconditional love from another person.

I tell engaged couples that it isn't only the grace of the Sacrament of Marriage that strengthens your relationship, but each time you have a child, the grace that comes from their baptism strengthens your marriage and family even more.

After thirty-two wonderful years of marriage, with all of the joys and the struggles that they have contained, we have learned the importance of taking advantage of all of the sacraments that the Church offers us. Though we have experienced times of anger and hurt in our relationship, the gift of repentance and the grace of the Sacrament of Reconciliation have brought healing and forgiveness to our life together. In receiving the Eucharist as often as possible, we experience the greatest source of grace for our life as a couple and as parents.

Within our marriage, through sickness, financial struggles, raising five children (with the challenges of the teenage years), experiencing the death of siblings and parents, and caring for elderly parents, we have discovered our need to call on God's grace. Even though the world tells us that long-lasting, happy marriages are not possible, the graces that God gives us through marriage and the other sacraments are more than strong enough to overcome all of these challenges. Not only can our marriages survive these struggles, but they can flourish and we can be witnesses to our children and to the world.

Questions for Couple and Group Discussion

1. In your own words, what is the difference between a covenant and a contract? Which better describes marriage?

2. Genesis 15:18 reads, literally, "It was on that occasion that the Lord *cut a covenant* with Abram ..." What is the significance of this phrase? What does it tell you about a covenant?

3. What two "parts" or "stages" of a covenant can be witnessed in Exodus 24:1–11?

4. Are there any parallels to these stages in Genesis 2:21–25?

5. What does the Church believe about the goodness of marriage (CCC 1604)?

6. Who is the primary actor in every sacrament (CCC 1088, 1127, 1509)?

7. How does the Church define sacraments (CCC 1084; see also 777, 1131)?

8. How many sacraments are there and what are their names (CCC 1113)?

9. What does the Church see as the cause of marriage (CCC 1626, 1627)?

10. Why must consent be free (CCC 1625, 1628)?

11. Who confers the Sacrament of Marriage (CCC 1623)?

12. What do couples promise to each other before God in their vows?

13. Who are the ministers of the sacrament in the view of the Western Church?

14. Why should marriage be celebrated as a public and ecclesial act (CCC 1631)?

15. What does "the language of the body" mean for Pope John Paul II, and how does it relate to the vows a couple exchanges?

16. The sacrament creates an unbreakable bond that is an ongoing source of grace for the couple (CCC 1640, 1642). How have you seen God's grace at work in your relationship thus far?

17. Name five things that you can do as a couple to consciously draw upon the grace available in the bond of marriage.

✠ Concluding Prayer ✠

Notes

6

Study Texts

GENESIS 3:1–4:1

1 Now the snake was the most cunning of all the wild animals that the LORD God had made. He asked the woman, "Did God really say, 'You shall not eat from any of the trees in the garden'?"

2 The woman answered the snake: "We may eat of the fruit of the trees in the garden;

3 it is only about the fruit of the tree in the middle of the garden that God said, 'You shall not eat it or even touch it, or else you will die.'"

4 But the snake said to the woman: "You certainly will not die!

5 God knows well that when you eat of it your eyes will be opened and you will be like gods, who know good and evil."

6 The woman saw that the tree was good for food and pleasing to the eyes, and the tree was desirable for gaining wisdom. So she took some of its fruit and ate it; and she also gave some to her husband, who was with her, and he ate it.

7 Then the eyes of both of them were opened, and they knew that they were naked; so they sewed fig leaves together and made loincloths for themselves.

8 When they heard the sound of the LORD God walking about in the garden at the breezy time of the day, the man and his wife hid themselves from the LORD God among the trees of the garden.

9 The LORD God then called to the man and asked him: Where are you?

10 He answered, "I heard you in the garden; but I was afraid, because I was naked, so I hid."

11 Then God asked: Who told you that you were naked? Have you eaten from the tree of which I had forbidden you to eat?

12 The man replied, "The woman whom you put here with me—she gave me fruit from the tree, so I ate it."

13 The LORD God then asked the woman: What is this you have done? The woman answered, "The snake tricked me, so I ate it."

14 Then the LORD God said to the snake:

> Because you have done this,
>
> cursed are you
>
> among all the animals, tame or wild;
>
> On your belly you shall crawl,
>
> and dust you shall eat
>
> all the days of your life.
>
> 15 I will put enmity between you and the woman,
>
> and between your offspring and hers;
>
> They will strike at your head,
>
> while you strike at their heel.

16 To the woman he said:

> I will intensify your toil in childbearing;
>
> in pain you shall bring forth children.
>
> Yet your urge shall be for your husband,
>
> and he shall rule over you.

17 To the man he said:

> Because you listened to your wife and ate from the tree about
>
> which I commanded you, You shall not eat from it,
>
> Cursed is the ground because of you!
>
> In toil you shall eat its yield
>
> all the days of your life.
>
> 18 Thorns and thistles it shall bear for you,
>
> and you shall eat the grass of the field.

19 By the sweat of your brow

you shall eat bread,

Until you return to the ground,

from which you were taken;

For you are dust,

and to dust you shall return.

20 The man gave his wife the name "Eve," because she was the mother of all the living.

21 The LORD God made for the man and his wife garments of skin, with which he clothed them.

22 Then the LORD God said: See! The man has become like one of us, knowing good and evil! Now, what if he also reaches out his hand to take fruit from the tree of life, and eats of it and lives forever?

23 The LORD God therefore banished him from the garden of Eden, to till the ground from which he had been taken.

24 He expelled the man, stationing the cherubim and the fiery revolving sword east of the garden of Eden, to guard the way to the tree of life.

4:1 The man had intercourse with his wife Eve, and she conceived and gave birth to Cain, saying, "I have produced a male child with the help of the LORD."

TOBIT 8:4–9

4 When Sarah's parents left the bedroom and closed the door behind them, Tobiah rose from bed and said to his wife, "My sister, come, let us pray and beg our Lord to grant us mercy and protection."

5 She got up, and they started to pray and beg that they might be protected. He began with these words:

"Blessed are you, O God of our ancestors;

blessed be your name forever and ever!

Let the heavens and all your creation bless you forever.

6 You made Adam, and you made his wife Eve

to be his helper and support;

and from these two the human race has come.

You said, 'It is not good for the man to be alone;
let us make him a helper like himself.'
7 Now, not with lust,
but with fidelity I take this kinswoman as my wife.
Send down your mercy on me and on her,
and grant that we may grow old together.
Bless us with children."
8 They said together, "Amen, amen!"
9 Then they went to bed for the night.

MATTHEW 5:27–28

27 "You have heard that it was said, 'You shall not commit adultery.'
28 But I say to you, everyone who looks at a woman with lust has already committed adultery with her in his heart."

REFLECTION

Genesis 3 recounts the disaster unleashed on the human race by the sin of our first parents. At the instigation of the serpent, the man and woman rebel against God's command and eat of the fruit of the tree of the knowledge of good and evil.[1] The Catholic Tradition sees in this original sin a disaster of cosmic proportions, resulting in the loss of original grace and justice not just for our first parents but for all of their descendants—us. Baptism removes the guilt of original sin, but not all of the disorder which it unleashed.

---

[1] Like many of the other features of the account (e.g., the garden, serpent), the "fruit" is symbolic and thus open-ended in the forms of disobedience that it can represent. This symbolic character does not undermine the profound theological truths communicated in our "revealed theological prehistory" as it is called by Saint John Paul II (see *Man and Woman He Created Them* 4:2 [September 26, 1979], p. 143). Like all of God's commands, the prohibition against eating it in Genesis 2:16–17 was understood by the people of Israel to indicate an invitation to a covenantal relationship with their Creator.

Even in the text, the consequences of Adam and Eve's rebellion are immediate and profound. Whereas in the previous chapter the man and woman were naked and unashamed (see Gen 2:25), they are now overtaken by shame and unable to remain unclothed before each other (Gen 3:7). Their shame and fear indicate a number of things. First, sin causes a profound rupture within the person so that his or her interior drives and desires are disordered. Saint John Paul II describes the Fall as "a certain constitutive fracture in the human person's interior, *a breakup, as it were, of man's original spiritual and somatic unity*."[2] Second, the openness and honesty of the couple's relationship symbolized in their naked bodies is damaged. Now they hide from and seek to deceive one another. Third, their shame and fear signifies the disordering of their sexual drives. Sexual union, in addition to being a means to ratify and recall the covenant of marriage, can now be a means to dominate and exploit others. Their naked bodies are now a sign of vulnerability.

God's adjudication of the couple in the dramatic scene at the end of the chapter brings home some of the further consequences of this sin. The snake (symbolic of the powers of evil) is reduced to crawling in the dirt. The relationship between man and woman is transformed from one of covenantal unity and equality to one of domination and subservience (Gen 3:16). Women will suffer pain in childbirth, work is infected by toil, and human beings are now subject to death—not just the cessation of biological life, but separation from the God who is the source of life.

But there are notes of hope sounded in this tragic story. Though the ground and the serpent are cursed, the man and woman are not. God's original blessing of the couple is not revoked, even though now it will primarily be realized in the procreation of new human life (see Gen 1:28, 4:1). East of Eden (see Gen 3:24), marriage will be lived in a diminished existence subject to struggle, sin, and death. But the text also gives a first intimation of Christ's victory in the Cross.[3] The powers of evil ("the seed

---

[2] *Man and Woman He Created Them*, 28:2 (May 28, 1980), pp. 243–44. Emphasis original.

[3] Many early Christians saw in Genesis 3:15 the *protoevangelium*—the first announcement of the Gospel message (CCC 410).

of the serpent")[4] will be defeated and will not have the final word over human life, love, and marriage.

Chapter 8 of the book of Tobit is one of the climactic points in the dramatic story it tells. Tobit's son Tobiah, who is on a mission to recover his family's wealth and bring healing to his blinded father, is joined in marriage to his cousin Sarah (whose previous seven husbands had been killed on their wedding night by a demon). They are delivered from this evil by their trust in God expressed in this magnificent prayer that recalls God's plan for marriage "from the beginning." Tobiah's motive in marrying his kinswoman is especially noteworthy—"not with lust but with [covenant] fidelity" (Tob 8:7). Marriage is ordered to covenant love as well as the gift of children, but in a fallen world the human heart is threatened by lust—one of the signs of the disorder unleashed by the Fall.

In the Old Testament, marriage is used as a covenant symbol to depict the relationship between Israel and God, but this use bears witness to the continued presence of sin in the world. Both idolatry and adultery, which are unique instances of covenant infidelity, are called "the great sin" in Old Testament texts (see Gen 20:9, 39:9; Ex 32 [referenced 3 times]; 2 Kings 17:21). Though God's plan for marriage was that it would be indissoluble, in Deuteronomy 24:1–4 Moses allowed men to divorce their wives if they found "something indecent" in them. Later, rabbis debated whether this permission required something like sexual infidelity or if it could be something as trivial as burning a dinner. Jesus, when asked about this debate (Mt 19:3), replies that Moses gave this law to the people because of their "hardness of heart" (Mt 19:8) and insists on marriage's unbreakable nature disclosed in the opening chapters of Genesis.

But Jesus doesn't just teach. As the New Moses, He not only clarifies the law and purifies His people's understanding of it, He also makes it possible in a radically new way. This is evident not only in His insistence on the indissolubility of marriage (Mt 5:31–32, 19:3–9; Mk 10:1–12; Lk

---

[4] As opposed to the seed of the woman, traditionally interpreted to be Jesus. The Hebrew text attributes "seed" (*zera*)—translated as "offspring" in the Study Texts above—to both the serpent and the woman.

16:18), but perhaps even more in His call to His disciples to have hearts free of the lust which is at the root of sexual infidelity (Mt 5:27–28). Humanly speaking, it is impossible to have a heart that is free of lust or of anger (see Mt 5:21–26), yet this is what Jesus calls us to have. How? It is worth recalling that the New Covenant spoken of by the prophets promised a transformation of the human heart. Jeremiah says that in the New Covenant the law would be written on the people's hearts (Jer 31:33) and that all of the people—from least to greatest—would know the Lord (Jer 31:34). Ezekiel states that in the New Covenant God would remove His people's "hearts of stone" and replace them with "a new heart and spirit" (Ezek 36:26). It is this that Jesus accomplishes in the victory of the Cross and the gift of the Holy Spirit. What is humanly impossible He makes possible. The human heart, divided by infidelity and riven by warring desires, can be made whole and capable of love. In Christ marriage is more than a symbol—it is a participation in the new life and transforming love that He gives. Marriage is thus a sacrament of healing.[5]

---

[5] The Catholic Tradition has frequently described marriage as a "remedy for concupiscence" (*remedium concupiscentiae*)—a remedy for the disorder created in us by sin.

Questions for Personal Reflection
and Couple Sharing

1. The Hebrew word for "snake" (*nachash*) in Genesis 3 can also be translated as "serpent" or "dragon." If the word is rendered "dragon," how might that change the way the text is read (Wisdom 2:24)?

2. Compare the woman's response to the serpent in Genesis 3:2 to the command God gave to the man in 2:16–17. What is different? What does this difference suggest about her trust in God's word to them?

3. Why is the man's silence while the evil serpent interrogates his wife problematic in light of God's directive to him to "cultivate [or guard] and care for" the garden (Gen 2:15)?

4. While a traditional association for fruit of the tree of the knowledge of good and evil is that it was an apple, there is no indication of that in the text. Instead the fruit is described as "good for food and pleasing to the eyes, and the tree was desirable for gaining wisdom" (Gen 3:6). What does this reveal about the nature of temptation and sin?

5. In Genesis 3:8 God is described as "walking about" in the Garden. The same term is used to describe His presence in the Temple tabernacle later in the Old Testament (see Lev 26:12; Deut 23:14; 2 Sam 7:6–7). What does this and other Temple imagery in Genesis 2 and 3 indicate about the nature of the Garden? What light does it shed on the couple's banishment?

6. Why is it important to read God's statement to the woman that her husband would "rule over" her as the result of sin and not God's original plan for the way the sexes relate?

7. Genesis 4:1 literally reads "the man *knew* [Hebrew: *yadah*] his wife Eve and she conceived and bore Cain, saying, 'I have produced a male child with the help of the LORD.'" What does this verb suggest that couples gain through sexual intercourse?

8. What does Tobiah's address of Sarah as "sister" (Tob 8:4) tell us about the relationship of husband and wife (see Song 4:9–10)?

9. What virtues do Tobiah and Sarah demonstrate in their wedding prayer together?

10. What are the three things for which Tobiah asks God in his marriage with Sarah?

11. Why does the Old Testament place idolatry and adultery in parallel? What does that indicate about the importance of marriage in God's plan for His people?

12. One of the places in Matthew's Gospel where Jesus is presented as the New Moses is the Sermon on the Mount (Mt 5–7). How does Matthew indicate this at the beginning of the Sermon (see Mt 5:1)?

13. To whom is the Sermon on the Mount addressed (see Mt 5:1–2)?

14. Matthew 5:21–48 is a series of antitheses in which Jesus cites a provision of the Law (the Decalogue or the Torah) and then radicalizes it in some way. How does he do this in relation to the 6th commandment in Matthew 5:27–28?

15. Name seven promises that Ezekiel's version of the promise of the New Covenant (Ezekiel 36:25–32) contains.

Notes

7

FOURTH SESSION

Nakedness, Love vs. Lust, the Gift of Children

OPENING

SCRIPTURE READING:

TOBIT 8:5–9

SUGGESTED PRAYER:

Blessed are You, O God of our ancestors; blessed be Your name forever and ever! Let the heavens and all your creation bless You forever. You made Adam, and You made his wife Eve to be his helper and support; and from these two the human race has come. You said, "It is not good for the man to be alone; let us make him a helper like himself." Let our marriages be permeated with Your mercy, fidelity, and love. Send down Your mercy on us, and grant that we may grow old together. Bless us with children and grandchildren.

CATECHETICAL REFLECTION

Created by God and created for the covenantal union of marriage, the human body in the state of original innocence could fully "speak" the reality of the person in all of his or her depth and uniqueness. As

Saint John Paul II says of the "nakedness" of our first parents described in Genesis 2:25: "'Nakedness' signifies the original good of the divine vision. It signifies the whole simplicity and fullness of this vision, which shows the 'pure' value of man as male and female, the 'pure' value of the body and [its] sex. . . . They see and know each other, in fact, with all the peace of the interior gaze, which creates precisely the fullness of the intimacy of persons."[1] Unclouded by the darkness of sin, the man and woman see each other as fully clothed in the dignity of their creation in the image and likeness of God (see Gen 1:27). They perceive both their common humanity and the personal difference which enables them to join as husband and wife.

They also perceive, much more profoundly than is possible for us in a fallen world, what it means to give their bodies to one another. To give one's body to another is to give oneself. St. John Paul II explains: "At the same time, they 'communicate' based on the communion of persons in which they become a mutual gift for each other, through femininity and masculinity. In reciprocity they reach in this way a particular understanding of the meaning of their own bodies."[2] As we saw in chapter 5, sexual intercourse is an action which completes and expresses the marriage covenant, communicating the promise of unconditional fidelity and the gift of oneself that a couple articulates in their wedding vows. This gift of self includes the totality of the person, including one's fertility. The blessing of children is one way in which the couple fulfills their vocation to exercise dominion over the earth given to them by God (see Gen 1:28).

Pope John Paul II thought that it was not accidental that the Hebrew Old Testament sometimes uses the term "knowledge" (*yada*) to describe sexual union in marriage. In giving oneself sexually, one comes to understand the meaning of one's own body as male or female and therefore to know the other more fully as husband or wife. But because fertility is an integral part of this gift, spouses also come to know each other as potential mother and father. Genesis 4:1 reveals this connection: "The man

---

[1] *Man and Woman He Created Them*, 13:1 (January 2, 1980), pp. 177–78.
[2] Ibid., 13:1 (January 2, 1980), p. 178.

had intercourse with his wife Eve, and she conceived and gave birth to Cain, saying, 'I have produced a male child with the help of the LORD.'" Commenting on this text, Saint John Paul II notes: "... we should observe that in Genesis 4:1 *the mystery of femininity manifests and reveals itself in its full depth through motherhood, as the text says, 'who conceived and gave birth.'* The woman stands before the man as mother, subject of the new human life that is conceived and develops in her and is born from her into the world. In this way, what also reveals itself is the mystery of man's masculinity, that is, the generative and 'paternal' meaning of his body."[3] The full meaning of the body and sexual union is seen in its ability to cooperate with God in the procreation of new human life. This is why the Church has always insisted that both faithfulness in the gift of self and openness to the blessing of children are integral to virtuous sexual union in marriage.

But "east of Eden" (Gen 3:24), where we find ourselves after the Fall, integrity in the gift of self and its meaning is a struggle. While called to the communion of love, we find our hearts pulled instead toward lust. Indeed, St. John Paul II taught that the human heart is often a battle-ground between love and lust—even among the followers of Jesus.[4]

What is the difference? Lust should not be understood as the same as sexual desire. God created us to be attracted to one another, as this is part of what draws us together in the union of marriage. Instead, lust is "inordinate" or disordered desire. Instead of desiring the other as a whole person—man or woman, made in the image of God—we see the other as an attractive object. The other is viewed as a "thing" for us to use and then discard rather than an integral person to be loved unconditionally. This can take the form of using the other for sexual pleasure or for emotional gratification. Many people are able to see some kinds of sexual conduct outside of marriage as expressions of lust: for example, adulterous sex,

---

[3] Ibid., 21:2 (March 12, 1980), pp. 210–11.
[4] See, for example, ibid., 39:3–4 (September 10, 1980), pp. 284–85. More characteristically in the Theology of the Body catecheses, St. John Paul II speaks of "disordered" or "inordinate" desire caused by the concupiscence of the flesh. The term "lust" is used here for purposes of simplicity.

commercialized sex such as prostitution, use of pornography, or solitary sexual practices such as masturbation. However, lust can also invade the hearts and relationships of those who are married as when a couple deliberately exclude the life-giving potential of sexual intercourse through some form of contraception or when one spouse engages in sexual practices which demean the other person.

The virtue that enables Christians to overcome the many forms of lust and live out their vocation to love is chastity. Chastity is not the same thing as continence or refraining from genital sex. Every Christian is called to chastity in their state of life—married, single, or celibate. Chastity takes our sexual drives and appetites and places them under the direction of our reason and will, as opposed to lust, which reverses this order. Chastity is the integration of oneself so that one can then freely give oneself in love—the self-possession which makes self-donation possible. A married couple in a passionate sexual relationship can be more chaste than an unmarried person who does not engage in sex out of fear or lack of opportunity. Conversely, sometimes chaste love within a marriage does require a couple to practice continence—as when they are separated by distance, recovering from illness or childbirth, or seek to devote themselves to prayer for a period of time (see 1 Cor 7:5). Married chastity ensures the couple's sexual relationship is governed by fidelity, respect for each other's dignity as persons, and reverence for its life-giving potential.

The Church also recognizes that for serious reasons couples can use some method of natural family planning (NFP) to avoid pregnancy for a period of time while continuing their sexual relationship. Natural family planning is fundamentally different from contraception. Even though it is as or more effective than most forms of contraception, it has none of the health risks they involve, it is not abortifacient (unlike some so-called "emergency contraceptives" or the IUD), and it can be used to enable couples (even those with limited fertility) to become pregnant, making it a real method of *family planning*. But there are deeper reasons for the moral difference between NFP and contraception. NFP sees fertility as an integral part of the person—not a disease to be suppressed through chemicals, devices, or surgery. Thus, on St. John Paul II's terms, NFP allows the "language of the body," of which sexual intercourse is part, to be spoken in truth in the couple's relationship. The practice of periodic continence during fertile periods when a couple is postponing pregnancy also strengthens the couple's growth in chastity and therefore their ability to communicate love. As Pope Francis observes: "Moreover, 'the use of methods based on the 'laws of nature and the incidence of fertility' (*Humanae vitae*, 11) are to be promoted, since 'these methods respect the bodies of the spouses, encourage tenderness between them and favor the education of an authentic freedom.' (*Catechism of the Catholic Church*, 2370)" (AL 222, citing the Final Report of the 2015 synod).

But the fact that the Church approves natural means of birth regulation should not obscure the fundamental teaching of Scripture and the Church's Tradition that children are a great gift. "Certainly sons are a gift from the LORD, the fruit of the womb, a reward," says the Psalmist (Ps 127:3), expressing the conviction of biblical sources from Genesis onward. The bishops of the Church gathered at the Second Vatican Council taught that: "By their very nature, the institution of matrimony itself and conjugal love are ordained for the procreation and education of children, and find in them their ultimate crown" (GS 48). In children, couples find a new and very tangible expression of their "one flesh" unity (see Gen 2:24). Children enrich a marriage in a myriad of ways, bringing their own unique gifts and personalities into the household and deepening the communion of love between the couple into a true community.

What of those who cannot have children? Saint John Chrysostom, the great preacher of the fourth-century East, says: "The child is a sort of bridge connecting the mother to the father, so that the three become one flesh, as when two cities divided by a river are joined by a bridge. But suppose there is no child; do they remain two and not one? No, their intercourse effects the joining of their bodies, and they are made one, just as when perfume is mixed with ointment."[5] No doubt drawing on his own pastoral work with couples who dealt with the cross of infertility, Saint

---

[5] St. John Chrysostom, *Homily 12 on Col 4:18*, in *On Marriage and Family Life*, 76.

John affirms that their sexual union still has value as the expression of a love and a union of persons. This remains the Church's understanding.

Couples who are physically infertile can realize the fruitfulness of marriage in a host of other ways. For example, when couples adopt a child, they realize the fruitfulness of their mutual love in a way that reflects God's generosity toward us in Christ, in us His adopted children (see Rom 8:15–17). Pope Francis cites a variety of other examples of this wider form of fruitfulness in addition to adoption: service to the wider society and Church, witness to their faith, care for the poor, treasuring the elderly, and supporting the isolated and the vulnerable (AL 178–97). Authentic love in a marriage always flows out from their relationship to enrich all of those around them.

Thoughts from Claire: NFP and the Gift of Children

When John and I got married, we were very young and John was just beginning graduate school so we thought it might be best to wait a little bit before having children. This turned out not to be God's plan for our family and our first daughter, Rachel Elizabeth, was born just before our first anniversary.

We were a bit anxious, wondering how we were going to raise a child in this busy time of our lives, but we were also excited at the thought of becoming parents. We knew that God had a plan for our family and that He would take care of us. It didn't take very long after Rachel's birth to begin to see what a wonderful blessing she was and how we were not just a couple, but a family. Instead of just being husband and wife, we were now mother and father. It really is amazing how being responsible for another tiny person caused us to mature and how she brought so much joy to our lives. Having children caused us to take our eyes off of ourselves and concentrate on caring for others. It was in serving and loving this little child that I came to know God's love for me in a deeper way. We were so blessed by this gift from God that we just couldn't wait to have another.

Again, we realized that God's plans aren't always the same as ours. It turned out to be difficult to conceive a second time. We actually had to take another NFP class in order to help us better understand our fertility in order to get pregnant again. This made us realize how precious life really is and how it is God who is the Author of all life. We can't just choose when we will have children or how many we will have. God knows what is best for each couple and each family.

Eventually, we were blessed with another daughter, Rebekah Anne, three years after Rachel was born. Since I don't have any sisters I was so happy that God had given us another beautiful little girl. Bekah was our miniature bundle of energy, always trying to keep up with her big sister. When I think back to those years when we were trying so hard to get pregnant (and worrying that we had secondary infertility), I realize that we wouldn't have had our precious little Bekah if we had gotten pregnant when we were planning. We would have never known this girl who brought so much joy and excitement to our family.

About sixteen months later we were expecting our third child. We had decided with each of our first four kids not to find out in advance what their gender was. Since I already had two girls, I told God that He could give me a boy if He wanted. Our first son, Paul Stephen, was born about two years after Bekah. He was such a peaceful and easy baby, I remember telling a friend with three sons that I didn't know boys were so wonderful and that I hoped we had more sons.

We now had three children and John was still in graduate school. We were young and had no money. We lived in a tiny apartment and couldn't imagine ever being able to buy a house. But we were filled with so much joy. God had blessed us with the gift of life and the great responsibility of sharing His love with these precious children. And God did provide us with what we needed to survive—through work, through the generosity of friends, and sometimes miraculously through anonymous gifts from others.

John finished his dissertation and was hired at the Catholic University of America in Washington, DC, three months after Paul was born. We moved to Maryland and ten months later found out that that we were expecting again. I was hoping for another boy. Eight years after we were married we were blessed with our second son Daniel John. Now we had four children and were amazed how each of them had a totally different personality and added a different dynamic to our family.

The next six years were filled with much joy and many challenges. We still struggled financially but tried to continue to trust that God would take care of us. We tried to seek His will for our family and were open to the gift of more children because we knew He would provide for us. John and I always dreamed of having a large family, maybe even eight to ten kids. We had started to have children early so it would be possible. But again, we discovered that God's plans are different than ours. It wasn't until six years after Daniel was born that we had our fifth child. Our whole family was excited when we found out that we were expecting again. Since we already had two girls and two boys, knowing how special and unique each one was, we weren't concerned with the sex of the baby. This time we decided to find out the baby's gender before birth, and all six of us went to the appointment to learn what God was giving us. We discovered that God was giving us another girl. The other kids helped us pick her name. We all liked the name Abigail, which means "the Father rejoices." We really believed that God was rejoicing that we were having another child. The two girls were in the delivery room to welcome their baby sister, Abigail Grace, into our family. I truly agree with Saint Teresa of Calcutta when she said that the greatest gift that you can give your children is siblings.

Questions for Couple and Group Discussion

1. What is the difference in the way in which our first parents experience nakedness before and after their sin (compare Gen 2:25 with 3:7)?

2. For John Paul II, though shame is the result of the Fall, it can have a positive function, reminding us of our dignity expressed in our bodies. How is the virtue of modesty connected to this?

3. What does it mean that to give one's body sexually is to give oneself as a person?

4. How is chastity "an apprenticeship in self-mastery" (see CCC 2339)?

5. Of which cardinal virtue does chastity form a part (CCC 2341)?

6. For Christians chastity is not just acquired through human effort and action, it is also a gift of grace. When do Christians first receive the infused virtues (CCC 2345)?

7. How does chastity vary in appearance in different Christian states of life? How is it nonetheless the same virtue?

8. What is the form of all other virtues in the Christian life (CCC 2346)? How does this virtue relate to marriage?

9. In your own words, how is the use of pornography (in or outside of a marriage) opposed to chastity (CCC 2354)?

10. What are the two meanings of the conjugal act according to Catholic teaching (CCC 2366)?

11. What are some of the key differences between natural family planning and contraception in the Church's understanding?

12. Why do both Scripture and the Church's Tradition see large families as a blessing?

13. Pope Francis teaches that "adoption is a very generous way to become parents" (AL 179). Why is this the case?

14. In what ways can science assist couples with limited fertility? What kinds of medical intervention does the Church oppose and why (CCC 2375–78)?

15. How are children a gift to their parents? To their siblings?

16. How does the experience of being a brother or sister within a family positively impact human society (AL 194–95)?

✳ Concluding Prayer ✳

Notes

8

Study Text

Ephesians 5:21-33

21 Be subordinate to one another out of reverence for Christ.

22 Wives should be subordinate to their husbands as to the Lord.

23 For the husband is head of his wife just as Christ is head of the church, he himself the savior of the body.

24 As the church is subordinate to Christ, so wives should be subordinate to their husbands in everything.

25 Husbands, love your wives, even as Christ loved the church and handed himself over for her

26 to sanctify her, cleansing her by the bath of water with the word,

27 that he might present to himself the church in splendor, without spot or wrinkle or any such thing, that she might be holy and without blemish.

28 So [also] husbands should love their wives as their own bodies. He who loves his wife loves himself.

29 For no one hates his own flesh but rather nourishes and cherishes it, even as Christ does the church,

30 because we are members of his body.

31 "For this reason a man shall leave [his] father and [his] mother and be joined to his wife,
and the two shall become one flesh."

32 This is a great mystery, but I speak in reference to Christ and the church.

33 In any case, each one of you should love his wife as himself, and the wife should respect her husband.

REFLECTION

This text in the fifth chapter of the Letter to the Ephesians is perhaps the best known of a group of passages in the New Testament that describe proper order in Christian households. Unfortunately, some modern readers see these texts as problematic because of their seeming insistence on the subordination of women to their husbands in marriage. This perception is troubling because it can lead to the neglect or dismissal of texts that contain profound teaching on marriage and the healing brought by Christ to the relationships within it. But to see this requires a careful reading of the text.

The passage begins with the exhortation to members of the Christian community: "be subordinate to one another out of reverence for Christ" (v. 21). The verb translated "be subordinate" (*hypotassomenoi*) has the connotation of an invitation directed to free persons (i.e., "freely subordinate yourselves . . .") as part of their commitment to the Lord. In the Greek text, there is actually no verb in verse 22, which is directed to wives. It literally says: "wives . . . to their husbands as to the Lord." This means that the verb is supplied by way of an ellipsis from verse 21 which indicates that grammatically it has to be read as connected to the exhortation given to all the members of the Christian community to be subject to one another.

The word for the "headship" of the husband in verse 23 is also significant. The Greek word used for "head" (*kephale*) when used elsewhere in St. Paul's letters usually means "source" as in an order of procession. So, for example, in 1 Corinthians 11:3 Paul writes: "But I want you to know that Christ is the head of every man, and a husband the head of his wife, and God the head of Christ." That text goes on to make clear that the Apostle has in mind the creation of woman from man in Genesis 2 (see 1 Cor 11:8–9). The same creation account underlies this teaching on marriage in Ephesians as the end of the chapter makes clear (see v. 31). When St. Paul teaches that "God is the head of Christ" he does not mean that the Christ is subordinate in the sense of being less than the Father or somehow secondary to Him, but rather that in the eternal communion of the Trinity the Son proceeds from the Father. So in the creation account the woman is created from man (Gen 2:18–23), yet the sexes are ultimately interdependent: "For just as woman came from man, so man is born of woman; but all things are from God" (1 Cor 11:12).

While women are enjoined to freely submit themselves to or "respect" (see Eph 5:33) their husbands, men are given a much more demanding directive. They are told to love their wives with the same love (v. 25: *agapate*) that Christ embodied in His sacrificial death on the Cross. Likewise, the term "handed over" (*paredoken*) is frequently used in the New Testament to refer to Christ's being "handed over" for us in the Passion. The Hellenistic world in which the Letter to the Ephesians was written was well acquainted with male domination of their wives and children within their households. Men were seen as the head in the sense of being the "boss" (*arche*), even in Roman law holding the power of life and death over children born within their households. The Letter to the Ephesians takes this concept of "headship" as domination and transforms it by overlaying it with the servant leadership of Christ who came not "to be served but to serve and to give his life as a ransom for many" (Mk 10:45). The husband is a leader within his marriage and family insofar as he lays down his life in loving service to his wife and children.

In so doing he fulfills the second half of the great commandment given by Christ in the Gospels, which is now applied to marriage: "husbands should love their wives as their own bodies. He who loves his wife loves himself" (Eph 5:28). A man's wife is his closest "neighbor," and he cannot respond to the teaching of Jesus if he fails to love her. The word "body" (*soma*) in verse 28 is followed by that for "flesh" (*sarx*) in the next verse. The use of both recalls the "one flesh/body" of Genesis 2:24 and brings the sacramental language of the text (the baptismal imagery of v. 26) into sharper focus by recalling the flesh of Christ given in the Eucharist through which He nourishes and sustains the Church (v. 29).

Receiving this flesh, the husband and wife are formed into members of the larger body of Christ (v. 30). The text therefore contributes to our understanding of a Christian marriage as a "domestic church"—a living cell of the larger Body of Christ in which He is present.

This Body of Christ in miniature, that is, a Christian marriage, is a "great mystery" (v. 32). The word *mysterion* is still used in Greek-speaking churches to describe the rites of the Church's worship celebrated in the liturgy. When the text was translated into Latin some four centuries later, the word chosen by Saint Jerome and others was *sacramentum*, which had the meaning of a sacred oath. The text thus forms a bridge between the understanding of marriage as a covenant found in the Old Testament and the later sacramental theology of the Church which would be fully articulated in the centuries to follow. Marriage is thus a mystery, a sacrament—an icon of God's love poured out in the New Covenant. In the "one flesh" union of a man and a woman joined to Christ in Baptism, the sacrificial love of Christ for the Church is lived and made visible in the world.

But what does this text teach concerning the relationship between the sexes? As we saw, one of the effects of sin described in Genesis 3 was the warping of relationships between men and women in marriage into one of (male) domination and (female) subservience: "your urge shall be for your husband, and he shall rule over you" (Gen 3:16). The fallen male impulse toward domination and exploitation of women is transformed by the sacrificial servant leadership of Christ. The fallen female impulse to either connive with this servile subjection or rebel against it is likewise overcome in the invitation directed to women as free persons to submit themselves to their husbands as an extension of their submission to Christ. While using language that would be intelligible in its first century context, Christian husbands and wives are called to remarkably similar responsibilities. For both, the invitation is to put their spouse and his or her needs ahead of their own, to defer to him or her in love, and to seek the good of the other rather than themselves. Some modern social scientists have observed that the specific language used to address each sex actually resonates with what contemporary men and women frequently describe as their primary relational needs: respect and acknowledgement for men, and being loved and cherished for women.[1]

The text of Ephesians thus highlights one of the specific ways in which Christ transforms and heals marriage. From a relationship marked by a warped pattern of domination and subservience in a fallen world, Christian marriage is meant to embody a pattern of relating in which each spouse lives for and seeks the good of the other ahead of their own interest. And this is not the result of their own willpower or effort—it is a gift of grace given by their incorporation into Christ. The same sacrificial love that He manifests in His death and communicates in the sacraments (*agapē*) is now the animating principle of their union. Christian marriage is indeed "a great mystery."

---

[1] This is not to say that men do not wish to be loved or that women do not wish to be respected—it is simply that they tend to prioritize these goods differently in marital relationships.

Questions for Personal Reflection
and Couple Sharing

1. Descriptions of proper order in households can be found in texts written by Jewish, Greek, and Roman authors. Typically in these texts, duties are only given to subordinate parties (e.g., women, children, slaves)—not to the male heads of households. What differences do you see in the following New Testament texts, and what do they tell us about the basic equality of women and men in Christ?

- "Wives, be subordinate to your husbands, as is proper in the Lord. Husbands, love your wives, and avoid any bitterness toward them" (Col 3:18–19).

- ". . . train younger women to love their husbands and children. . . . Urge the younger men, similarly, to control themselves" (Tit 2:4, 6).

- "Likewise, you wives should be subordinate to your husbands so that, even if some disobey the word, they may be won over without a word by their wives' conduct when they observe your reverent and chaste behavior. . . . Likewise, you husbands should live with your wives in understanding, showing honor to the weaker female sex, since we are joint heirs of the gift of life, so that your prayers may not be hindered (1 Pet 3:1–2, 7).

2. A similar reciprocity and mutual respect is meant to characterize the relationship between Christian parents and children. What do the following texts teach in this regard?

- "Children, obey your parents [in the Lord], for this is right. 'Honor your father and mother.' This is the first commandment with a promise, 'that it may go well with you and that you may have a long life on earth.' Fathers, do not provoke your children to anger, but bring them up with the training and instruction of the Lord" (Eph 6:1–4).

- "Children, obey your parents in everything, for this is pleasing to the Lord. Fathers, do not provoke your children, so they may not become discouraged" (Col 3:20–21).

3. The word for the love of husbands for their wives in verse 25 is *agapē*. What do the following texts teach about this love and its source?

- John 3:35

- John 10:17

- John 13:35

- John 15:9, 17

- 1 John 3:1

- 1 John 3:16

- 1 John 4:7–12

- 1 John 4:20–21

4. Read 1 Corinthians 13:4–13. List seven qualities of love described in the text. How might each of these apply to a Christian marriage?

Quality	Application
_____	_____
_____	_____
_____	_____
_____	_____
_____	_____
_____	_____
_____	_____

5. What are the two parts of the Great Commandment given by Jesus to his followers according to Luke 10:25–28?

6. How are these two parts illustrated in Luke 10:29–42?

7. What is the image that St. Paul uses to describe the interdependence of the members of the Church in 1 Corinthians 12:12–31?

8. How is this image present in Ephesians 5:28–30 and what does this tell us about the relationship of the Christian couple to the Church?

9. How does Christ nourish and sustain the Church (Eph 5:29)?

10. What does it mean that marriage is "a great mystery"?

11. List four concrete ways a husband or wife can show respect to their spouse.

12. List four concrete ways spouses can demonstrate their love for one another.

Notes

FIFTH SESSION

Mutual Submission: Church Teaching and Practice

OPENING

SCRIPTURE READING:

COLOSSIANS 3:18–21

SUGGESTED PRAYER:

God our Father, You willed that Christian marriage would be a reflection of the love that unites Your Son to His bride, the Church. Help us to understand and live our vocation in such a way that Your love is made visible in the world. Teach us to live for one another and to put each other's needs ahead of our own. Help us to use our gifts for the good of each other and our families.

CATECHETICAL REFLECTION

In receiving the biblical witness, the early Church inherited what seem to be conflicting impulses concerning the relation of the sexes. On the one hand, the Gospels recount the countercultural ways Jesus related to women—including them amongst the recipients of His teaching, healing, and exorcisms; making them the first witnesses to His Resurrection; and even numbering them among His own disciples. Saint Paul affirms the fundamental equality of women and men as baptized members of the Body of Christ (Gal 3:27–28). On the other hand, women were not numbered among the Apostles, were somewhat restricted in their participation in liturgical worship (see 1 Cor 14:34–35), and were seemingly given distinct roles within the Christian household with husbands as heads of their families. In the centuries that followed, the Church sought to balance these impulses—a recognition of the equal dignity of women and men as called to salvation, while viewing them as having distinct gifts and roles. And all of this took place within specific cultural contexts that colored the way they were understood and lived out.

So Saint John Chrysostom, the great fourth-century preacher, taught in his homilies that a Christian household cannot be a democracy. Men and women have distinct gifts and roles that are meant to function in unison for the good of their family and the Church. Men exercise their gifts primarily in the public forum—in military and political affairs, council chambers, and the market. Women's domain is within the household—managing servants, children, and household affairs. Using Saint Paul's image, he describes the husband's role as that of the "head," while the wife's role is that of the "body." Men are called to love their wives (which he believes to be the more demanding responsibility) while women are called to obey their husbands.[1] However, Saint John makes some important qualifications. Neither spouse is excused from their responsibility if the other is delinquent—a husband must still love a disobedient wife and a wife must still obey an unloving husband (though not to the point of sin). Both husbands and wives are called to teach each other and their children virtue by word and example. The key, for Chrysostom, is using these distinct roles to build harmonious cooperation in the home.

The women's movements of the nineteenth and twentieth centuries, which sought for and achieved greater political rights and social and economic participation for women, have spurred the Church to ponder the

---

[1] See St. John Chrysostom, *Homily 20 on Ephesians 5:22–33*, in *On Marriage and Family Life*, 43–64.

biblical witness anew. The result in the twentieth and twenty-first centuries has been a development of the Church's teaching on marriage as it pertains to the roles of men and women in the family.

The beginning of this development can be seen in the teaching of Pope Pius XI in his Encyclical Letter on Christian Marriage *Casti connubii* (1930). Reflecting on the New Testament teaching regarding men being the heads of their households, the pope offered an important distinction. While men enjoy primacy in the order of authority, women enjoy primacy in the order of love, and so exercise leadership within their homes, albeit of a different kind: "For if the man is the head, the woman is the heart, and as he occupies the chief place in ruling, so she may and ought to claim for herself the chief place in love."[2]

However, the key development in the Church's understanding was put forward by Saint John Paul II. The Polish pope taught extensively about the family and about the dignity and gifts of women in society and in the Church. In his Apostolic Letter *Mulieris dignitatem* (1988), he offered an extended commentary on the teaching of Saint Paul in Ephesians 5:21–6:4. Admitting to a certain cultural influence in the way the exhortations directed to men and women are framed ("wives be subordinate to your husbands"), he insists on the revolutionary character of the teaching. In light of the whole of the biblical witness and the Church's deepening understanding of the dignity of the sexes, the text must be read and understood in a new way: "All the reasons in favor of the 'subjection' of woman to man in marriage must be understood in the sense of a 'mutual subjection' of both 'out of reverence for Christ.'"[3]

He bases this reading of the biblical text on a number of factors. First, the text itself begins with an injunction to mutual submission: "Be subordinate to one another out of reverence for Christ" (Eph 5:21). Second, he says, this language captures the "style" of Jesus in the Gospels of always relating to women as persons rather than being constrained by

---

[2] Pope Pius XI, Encyclical Letter on Christian Marriage *Casti connubii* (December 31, 1930), §27.

[3] Pope St. John Paul II, Apostolic Letter on the Dignity and Vocation of Women *Mulieris dignitatem* (August 15, 1988), §24.

cultural expectations of how rabbis should have no dealings with women. Third, he appeals to the "ethos of the Gospel" concerning the dignity of all persons, which the Church is now understanding more deeply in its application to women. He notes that something similar can be observed in regard to slavery (referenced at the end of the text—see Eph 6:5–9). As it took centuries for the Church to recognize the incompatibility of the dignity of the human person with the practice of slavery, so the Church, in pondering the revelation entrusted to Her, has now come to a deeper understanding of the mutual authority exercised by Christian spouses in marriage.

The ultimate ground for this teaching was articulated by "the Pope of the family" in his Theology of the Body catecheses some years earlier. If both a husband and a wife are submitted to Christ as the "head" of their relationship and home (as Eph 5:21 enjoins), then there can be no servile subjection to one another. The only true "head" of a Christian marriage is Christ. The reverence for Christ (*pietas*) which spouses have leads them to submit themselves to each other in love.[4] The differing temperaments and gifts of men and women must be placed at the service of each other to build up the domestic church, which is their home.

Pope Francis reaffirms this teaching of his predecessor and extends it to the sexual relationship of the Christian couple:

> Every form of sexual submission must be clearly rejected. This includes all improper interpretations of the passage in the Letter to the Ephesians where Paul tells women to 'be subject to your husbands' (*Eph* 5:22). This passage mirrors the cultural categories of the time, but our concern is not with its cultural matrix but with the revealed message that it conveys. As Saint John Paul II wisely observed: 'Love excludes every kind of subjection whereby the wife might become a servant or a slave of the husband. . . . The community or unity which they should establish through marriage is constituted by a reciprocal donation of

---

[4] See *Man and Woman He Created Them*, 89:1–8 (August 11, 1982), pp. 472–75.

self, which is also a mutual subjection.' Hence Paul goes on to say that 'husbands should love their wives as their own bodies' (*Eph* 5:28). . . . In marriage, this reciprocal 'submission' takes on a special meaning, and is seen as a freely chosen mutual belonging marked by fidelity, respect and care. Sexuality is inseparably at the service of conjugal friendship, for it is meant to aid the fulfilment of the other. (AL 156)

It is on this basis that one can understand the evil of abuse—whether emotional, physical, or sexual—when it takes place within marriage. Thus the Church continues to uphold the equal dignity of women and men as human and as baptized, but her understanding of the mutual exercise of authority between them in their diverse gifts has developed in the recent teaching of the magisterium.

What does this teaching mean? First of all, it does not mean—as some might worry—some rupture with the Church's previous teaching in this area. Authentic development of doctrine is never a complete break with the previous Tradition. Rather, doctrinal development re-presents previous teaching in a fuller and more adequate context. In this case, there is no abandonment of the idea that wives are called to submit to their husbands. Instead, this teaching is balanced by the insistence that men are in turn called to submit themselves to their wives in love. This new formulation provides a better reading of the text of Ephesians (beginning as it does with the exhortation to mutual submission in 5:21); it gives deeper insight into the equal dignity of the spouses which the Church has always affirmed; and it gives the spouses a vision of Christian marriage as living for the good of the other. In this way spouses reflect the eternal communion of love of the Persons of the Trinity, witnessed in the economy of salvation where each of the Divine Persons seeks the glory of the others.

The practical import of this development in the Church's understanding of marriage is that the heart of Christian marriage is not wielding power, but love, self-sacrifice, and service. Men and women, with all of their different gifts and inclinations as well as their distinctive personalities, are called to live for each other, putting their spouse's good ahead of their own. Ultimately, this is what the language of free submission to another or Christlike sacrificial love envisions in language that would be intelligible to first-century Christians living within the Roman empire. Yet, some social scientists have observed that the language of "respect" shown to husbands by their wives and "love" shown to wives by their husbands actually corresponds to the relational needs prioritized by many twenty-first century men and women.[5] This mutual deference requires open and honest communication.

An example of what mutual submission might look like in daily married life can be seen in the case of a couple using some version of natural family planning to live out the Church's teaching regarding responsible parenthood. A couple must communicate and prayerfully decide together whether they are seeking to conceive children together or postpone pregnancy due to serious reasons. All of their differences as men and women and as individuals enter into this process of communication, discernment, and decision-making. They then have to monitor their shared fertility and express their love in ways that reflect their shared decision—that is, expressing love in non-sexual ways when they are fertile if they are seeking to postpone pregnancy, or prioritizing sexual intercourse during fertile periods if they are seeking to become pregnant. Using natural family planning thus requires couples to communicate and make decisions together in a way that embodies the Church's vision of mutual submission in marriage.

All this is to say that "mutual submission" is not new or outside the experience of most Christian married couples. In any good marriage where couples communicate, listen to one another, and willingly sacrifice to seek the other's good, there is some version of mutual submission out of reverence for Christ (see Eph 5:21) at work.

---

[5] See, for example, Emerson Eggerichs, *Love and Respect: The Love She Most Desires; The Respect He Desperately Needs* (Nashville, TN: Thomas Nelson, 2004).

THOUGHTS FROM CLAIRE: MUTUAL SUBMISSION

When we first got married, John was in charge of all of our finances. Every month, he would work on a budget and try to pay all of our bills. We both just assumed that this was what a husband was supposed to do. He would get stressed out trying to figure out how to pay the bills with the little bit of income that we had, and I would spend our money on things I thought we needed. He became frustrated and just didn't know what to do. He went to prayer and begged God to give him wisdom in this situation. He felt that God told him to let me take over the finances for a while and I trusted this decision.

I started doing our finances shortly after our first anniversary. This was one of the best decisions we ever made. John had more time for his studies, and I became aware of how little money we really had. It was during this time that we discovered I had talents that we hadn't been aware of previously. I became a very frugal person, able to find the best deals on necessary items. I learned to live more simply when I realized that we didn't need everything I thought we did. I also developed a greater trust in God's provision for us.

There were so many times that we prayed for miracles, and God always took care of us. Often this was through the generosity of others— both known and unknown. We received an anonymous gift of $1,000 from a benefactor of Marquette's graduate program; this enabled us to buy our first computer. We had friends who would buy a half a cow for their freezer each year who would give us all of their leftover beef, ena- bling us to eat steaks and burgers while on a graduate student's budget.

About six years ago, we decided to take one of Dave Ramsey's Finan- cial Peace classes when it was offered at our parish. This class really helped our marriage by giving us tools to use our money more wisely and in the service of God. Even though I am still the one who pays the bills and finds the good deals, we now take time to plan our budget together. We decide together how God wants us to spend and save our money and where and how much to tithe. This has not only brought us much peace but has brought us closer together and improved our communication in the area of finances.

Over the years we have discovered that we have different gifts that we can use to help our family. We've learned not to stereotype which jobs and decisions are for the wife and which are for the husband. Since John worked in a hospital as a janitor through college and graduate school, he became very good at cleaning. He is more particular about how we clean and which cleaning products we use, so I buy whatever he likes. John has taught all of our children how to clean and do laundry. When the kids lived at home, starting at a very young age, we would have family cleaning days on which we all worked together to clean the house. They also helped out in the yard. Everyone learned how to mow the lawn and to plant and weed the gardens. I love to cook and had our children help me cook dinners and do baking for the holidays. Today, all of our children, including our sons, are good cooks.

Of course, there are areas of responsibility that can't be delegated, but need to be done together, like raising children and teaching the Faith. When the children were little and I was the one home with them all day, I did most of the daily disciplining. I was the primary one who read them books on the lives of the saints and took them to daily Mass with me to familiarize them with the blessings of our Faith. As they got older, especially during the teenage years, it became more important for John to help me teach them the Faith. He would use the Catechism and talk to them about different issues facing the Church and our culture. We both tried to evangelize and be witnesses to them on a daily basis. During their adolescence, we also had to work together as disciplining grew more challenging.

I think that the greatest gift that we have given our children is showing them that we love and respect each other and desire to serve our family together. We have tried to show them the importance of praying and discerning together to know God's will for our family and for their lives. Since we differ in certain areas as a couple, we have also tried to teach them that we can still work through life together, trusting that God is guiding us and will help us to do the right thing.

Questions for Couple and Group Discussion

1. How is the exercise of authority in marriage disturbed by the sin of our first parents (see Gen 3:16)?

2. How does mutual submission out of reverence for Christ (see Eph 5:21) represent the healing of this disorder?

3. What is the purpose of authority in the understanding of the Church (CCC 1897)?

4. How does Jesus exercise His authority (see Mk 10:45)?

5. How do the different roles of family members impact their dignity vis-à-vis each other (CCC 2203)?

6. List three duties of children toward their parents (CCC 2214–20).

7. List three duties of parents for their children (CCC 2221–31).

8. List three duties of spouses toward one another.

9. What do the following texts teach about the aim of the Divine Persons in the work of our salvation?
- John 8:50

- John 8:54

- John 14:13

- John 16:14

- John 17:1–5

10. List three things that your spouse/fiancée has done that demonstrated his/her respect for you in the last month.

11. List three things that your spouse/fiancée has done that demonstrated sacrificial love for you in the last month.

12. Why does mutual submission require communication on the part of a couple?

13. One way that mutual submission functions in marriage is when husbands and wives recognize each other's gifts and delegate certain responsibilities to each other. Give two examples where you see this functioning in your own relationship.

14. There are other areas of a couple's life too important to delegate and make the sole responsibility of one spouse. Give two examples of these areas and explain why you think this to be the case. If your examples differ from those of your fiancée or spouse, discuss this with each other.

15. Can you think of a time when you disagreed on a specific issue, but after discussion, thought, and prayer, agreed with your fiancée or spouse? What caused you to change your mind in this case?

✴ Concluding Prayer ✴

Notes

10

Study Texts

COLOSSIANS 3:12–17

12 Put on then, as God's chosen ones, holy and beloved, heartfelt compassion, kindness, humility, gentleness, and patience,

13 bearing with one another and forgiving one another, if one has a grievance against another; as the Lord has forgiven you, so must you also do.

14 And over all these put on love, that is, the bond of perfection.

15 And let the peace of Christ control your hearts, the peace into which you were also called in one body. And be thankful.

16 Let the word of Christ dwell in you richly, as in all wisdom you teach and admonish one another, singing psalms, hymns, and spiritual songs with gratitude in your hearts to God.

17 And whatever you do, in word or in deed, do everything in the name of the Lord Jesus, giving thanks to God the Father through him.

EPHESIANS 4:25–27

25 Therefore, putting away falsehood, speak the truth, each one to his neighbor, for we are members one of another.

26 Be angry but do not sin; do not let the sun set on your anger,

27 and do not leave room for the devil.

REFLECTION

The two texts under consideration here have special application to the Christian household as a living cell of the larger Body of Christ.

In the case of the first, from St. Paul's Letter to the Colossians, the text itself signals this relevance. The third chapter of the letter opens with a reminder to the Christians of Colossae of ideas found elsewhere in Paul's teaching (Col 3:1–11). As Christians, they are dead to sin through Baptism (see Rom 6:2–5) and are called to separate themselves from vices characteristic of those dominated by the power of sin (see Rom 1:29–31; Gal 5:19–21). Such vices include: "immorality, impurity, passion, evil desire, and the greed that is idolatry" (Col 3:5) as well as "anger, fury, malice, slander, and obscene language" and "lying" (see 3:8–9). It ends with a passage very similar to the household order text of Ephesians 5:21–6:4 (see Col 3:18–25). Given new life in Baptism, Christians are called to foster this new life in the Church and in the domestic church, which is the household.

The section that lies in between the beginning and end of the chapter (vv. 12–17 of chapter 3) describes the new identity that Christians are given in the body of Christ and the practices and virtues they need to live it out. The Colossian Christians are described by St. Paul with a series of terms that recall God's covenant people in the Old Testament. They are "chosen" or "elect" (*eklektoi*), "holy" (*hagioi*) and "beloved" (ēgapēme-noi)—all terms applied to the people of Israel in the Greek translation of the Hebrew Old Testament. These believers are thus part of the New Israel established by Jesus and are called to relate to each other as such. As opposed to the vices which they are told to shun, they are called instead to practice virtues of "compassion, kindness, humility, gentleness, and patience" (v. 12). They are called to cultivate peace (identified elsewhere by St. Paul as one of the "fruits of the Holy Spirit"—Gal 5:22) and to be "thankful" (*eucharistoi*), meditating on Scripture and the music used in their liturgical worship (vv. 15–17). The threefold use of the phrase "one another" injects a note of mutuality into the text, indicating that these are responsibilities of all members of the community in relation to each other. It also injects a note of mutuality into the exhortation directed to members of households that follows (vv. 18–25), not unlike the formulation of Ephesians 5:21.

But at the heart of the practices and virtues this text holds up for the Christian community, including its households, St. Paul underscores two things—mutual forgiveness and love. As they have been forgiven in Christ, the Christians of Colossae are called to forgive each other. This is, after all, what Christians petition for in the Lord's Prayer (see Mt 6:12). As they have been loved in Christ, they are called to love. Love, for St. Paul, is "the bond of perfection" (Col 3:14). It is that which perfects all of these other virtues and practices, making them complete and life-giving. It is love (*agapē*), which is the summit of Christian life, lasting even to the vision of God where faith and hope have passed away (1 Cor 13). It is this love that St. Paul calls Christian husbands to manifest to their wives at the end of this chapter (Col 3:19) and in Ephesians 5. In this way, Christian marriage and families can conform themselves to Christ and the new life they receive from Him both in "word or in deed" (v. 17).

The brief text from Ephesians 4 expands upon the exhortation to mutual forgiveness at the heart of community life found in Colossians. It is no accident that the Church includes most of this brief text as the reading for night prayer every Wednesday.

Verse 25 enjoins members of the Christian community to practice honesty. Colossian 3:9 named "lying" as one of the vices that baptized believers are called to put off. Here Saint Paul echoes the prophet Zechariah describing the requirements of justice: "Speak the truth to one another" (Zech 8:16). The reason the Apostle supplies is that "we are members one of another" (Eph 4:25). This recalls Saint Paul's image of the Church as the body of Christ in which all members are interdependent parts of that larger whole (see 1 Cor 12, 14). It is impossible to live in a community where all members depend on each other if there is deception and lying, as these destroy trust and confidence in others.

But perhaps even more destructive to Christian community than lying is resentment. Our English word "resentment" comes from the Old French word *resentir*—"to feel again." The person who resents another feels again and again the pain of some injury (real or imagined) that dominates his or her heart and strangles his or her ability to love. It is a poison in the heart that corrodes the capacity to relate to others in a community.

Verse 26 of chapter 4 invokes Psalm 4:5: "Tremble and sin no more." The Hebrew word here for "tremble" is *rigzū*, which means to tremble in religious fear or awe. However, when the Old Testament was translated from Hebrew to Greek, the word was understood in the sense of the trembling caused by anger, and this is how St. Paul understands it here. Christians are enjoined to be angry yet without sin. How is such righteous anger possible? The text recommends immediate (i.e., daily) reconciliation: "do not let the sun set on your anger" so that Satan does not have the opportunity to ensnare a believer in sin or in the spiritually destructive trap of resentment.

If deception and resentment are destructive of the bonds of love that unite the members of the Christian community to one another, this is true also of the Christian community that shares life together in a household. It is worth recalling that in the early decades of the Church's life, in which Saint Paul lived and wrote, local Christian communities generally did not have buildings set aside for worship. Instead they often met in homes of believers, giving rise to the expression "house" or "domestic" churches (see Acts 12:12, 16:40; Rom 16:3, 16:5; Col 4:15; Philem 1–2). Married couples and families would do well to ponder texts such as these from Colossians 3 and Ephesians 4 as basic rules for their life together.

Questions for Personal Reflection and Couple Sharing

1. How does the Church understand virtue (CCC 1803)?

2. What is the difference between human and infused virtues (CCC 1804, 1810, 1812)?

3. What are the four cardinal virtues (CCC 1805–9)? Why are they called "cardinal"?

4. What are the three theological virtues (CCC 1814–26)? Which is the most important?

5. Which of these seven virtues are most necessary for a Christian household and why?

6. Name three other virtues (not among these seven) that are especially important for a Christian marriage and family.

7. What are the seven fruits of the Holy Spirit (Gal 5:22–23; CCC 1832)?

8. What kind of practices or resources help one to grow in virtue (CCC 1810, 1811, 1839)?

9. What are the seven deadly (or capital) sins (CCC 1866)?

10. Read or recite the Our Father (see Mt 6:9–13). What are the seven petitions the Lord's Prayer contains (CCC 2803–6)?

11. How do these petitions correspond to the seven central virtues of the Christian life (CCC 1805, 1841)?

12. What is the difference between righteous and sinful anger (CCC 2302)?

13. Can you give an example of righteous anger in Scripture or from your own life?

14. The letter of James counsels: "Know this, my dear brothers: everyone should be quick to hear, slow to speak, slow to wrath, for the wrath of a man does not accomplish the righteousness of God" (1:19–20). How does this text supplement St. Paul's exhortation in Colossians 3:13 and Ephesians 4:26–27?

15. What is the role of parents in the domestic church (CCC 1656)?

16. How is the priesthood of the baptized exercised in a Christian household (CCC 1657)?

Notes

11

The Forms of Intimacy in a Healthy Marriage

OPENING

SCRIPTURE READING
1 PETER 3:7–9

SUGGESTED PRAYER:

Lord, You are the author of all love. Thank You for the love that has drawn us together. Help us to cherish and nurture that love in our daily lives and interaction with one another. Help us to never take each other or our relationships for granted. Teach us to treasure our time together, to listen to one another, and to work through conflict with each other so that we can grow in the gift of Your love.

CATECHETICAL REFLECTION

When people in our culture think of the word "intimacy," very often the first thing that comes to their minds is sex. If someone says that two people have an "intimate relationship," that person typically means that the couple is sexually active. Men in particular tend to focus on sex as identical to or at the center of intimacy in a relationship.

Yet, reflection shows intimacy and sex are not the same thing. One can have a close friendship or deep connection with another person without any sexual expression. This is true of most close friendships. Conversely, our culture is awash in sexual practices and behaviors in which there is no real intimacy (e.g., pornography consumption or commercial sex, such as strip clubs or prostitution). So it is possible to have intimacy without sex and sex without intimacy.

Marriage is a unique form of friendship that involves the full range of human experience and intimacy. In his encyclical *Humanae vitae*, Pope Paul VI describes marriage as animated by a love that is "fully human, a compound of sense and spirit." It is, he says, "a love which is total—that very special form of personal friendship in which husband and wife generously share everything."[1] The distinctive aspect of married love that transcends friendship is that it involves a unique unity of persons, based on the gift of one's whole self. As John Paul II expresses it in *Familiaris consortio*: "conjugal love involves a totality, in which all the elements of the person enter—appeal of the body and instinct, power of feeling and affectivity, aspiration of the spirit and of will. It aims at a deeply personal unity, the unity that, beyond union in one flesh, leads to forming one heart and soul; it demands indissolubility and faithfulness in definitive mutual giving; and it is open to fertility" (FC 13).

Social scientists and marriage counselors describe multiple forms of intimacy necessary for a healthy marriage—verbal/emotional, physical, spiritual, and sexual. Many of these forms of intimacy are impacted by the differences between the sexes as well as by individual personality types and family history. So, for example, in regard to verbal and emotional intimacy, which is developed and sustained through communication, men and women tend to have different approaches or "styles." Men tend to be more focused on communication, aimed at imparting practical information, and attempting to fix problems. This, of course, has given rise to the image in both scientific discussion and comedy circles of hus-

---

[1] Pope Paul VI, Encyclical Letter on the Regulation of Birth *Humanae vitae* (July 25, 1968), §9.

bands as "Mr. Fix It" or the "Toolman" within the household. Women, with greater connection between the hemispheres of their brains,[2] are not only generally better at multitasking than men, but better at integrating feelings as well as information in their communication, and seek to build and sustain interpersonal connection. As one researcher puts it, men tend to aim at "report" in their communication style, while women tend to foster "rapport."[3] These differences as well as others can pose challenges to couples in their effort to build intimacy through effective communication.

Physical intimacy is not the same as sex. In fact, couples whose only physical contact is sexual in nature often suffer from an overall lack of intimacy in their relationship. Rather, physical intimacy refers to all of the physical—but not overtly sexual—forms of physical touch and affection in a marriage: holding hands, giving back or foot rubs, tending to the other person while he or she is recovering from illness, etc.

Spiritual intimacy is one of the most important but often most neglected forms of intimacy in marriage. This dimension of a couple's closeness is built through sharing their lives of faith with one another. They can do this by praying together, attending liturgical worship together, or by studying and sharing about Scripture or Church teaching with each other. Couples can also encourage and support each other in developing a regular prayer life and sharing the fruit of it with one another. In many ways, this is the deepest part of marital intimacy insofar as in it men and women share the One who is, in the beautiful words of St. Augustine, "higher than my highest and more inward than my innermost self."[4] Spiritual intimacy enables the whole of a couple's life and all of the forms of intimacy lived out in their daily life together to become

---

[2] On this and other biological differences in brain structure between the sexes which impact behaviour, see Louann Brizendine, *The Female Brain* (New York: Broadway Books, 2006), 4–7, 91–92.

[3] See Deborah Tannen, "Put Down that Paper and Talk to Me!" in Kieran Scott and Michael Warren, eds., *Perspectives on Marriage*, 3rd ed. (Oxford, UK: Oxford University, 2006), 244–59.

[4] St. Augustine, *Confessions* III, 6, 11. Quoted in Pope Benedict XVI, Angelus Message, December 11, 2011, http://w2.vatican.va/content/benedict-xvi/en/angelus/2011/documents/hf_ben-xvi_ang_20111211.html.

an extension of the "liturgical language" of their wedding vows (see AL 215).[5]

These three dimensions of intimacy form the context and indispensable backdrop for sexual expression in marriage, making it a vehicle to communicate their closeness and affection for one another. Sexual intimacy, in turn, acts as a mirror, reflecting back the closeness or connection in other parts of a couple's life and relationship—or the lack thereof. Sometimes when couples seek help from a counselor or doctor because of "sexual problems," there is actually no physiological problem affecting their sexual relationship. Instead, it can be things like a failure of communication, unresolved conflict, or a lack of other kinds of physical touch that are disrupting the sexual expression in their relationship. Further confirming this mirroring character of sex in marriage, studies have found couples who regularly pray together tend to enjoy their sexual relationship far more than couples who do not.[6]

Sustaining intimacy over time takes work on the part of couples. And there are points in a marriage when this is especially important. One of these is relatively early on in a marriage when the initial "glow" has faded from the relationship. Often this happens at around the five- to seven-year mark, but it can happen earlier as well. Pope Francis wisely observes in regard to the early stages of marriage:

> This process takes time. Love needs time and space; everything else is secondary. Time is needed to talk things over, to embrace leisurely, to share plans, to listen to one other and gaze in each other's eyes, to appreciate one another and to build a stronger relationship. Sometimes the frenetic pace of our society and the pressures of the workplace create problems. At other times, the problem is the lack of quality time together, sharing the same room without one even noticing the other. . . . [Experienced couples] can also provide resources that help young married

---

[5] See also *Man and Woman He Created Them*, 117b (July 4, 1984), pp. 613–15.

[6] See, example, Fr. Andrew Greeley, *Faithful Attraction: Discovering Intimacy, Love, and Fidelity in American Marriage* (New York: St. Martin's, 1991).

couples to make those moments meaningful and loving, and thus to improve their communication. This is extremely important for the stage when the novelty of marriage has worn off. Once a couple no longer knows how to spend time together, one or both of them will end up taking refuge in gadgets, finding other commitments, seeking the embrace of another, or simply looking for ways to flee what has become an uncomfortable closeness. (AL 224–25)

Another common time when couples often feel more distant from each other is when they hit the "empty nest" phase of their family life. A couple who has invested all of their time and energy in parenting but neglected their own relationship can find themselves unsure of how to reconnect and move forward with each other in this new phase of their life.

What steps can couples take to build and sustain intimacy, especially during difficult periods during which they feel less close? Marriage counselors and social scientists highlight a number of things as "best practices" in this regard. It is important that couples prioritize regular (i.e., daily) time set aside for communication without the demands of kids or media to distract them. This communication involves not only talking, but active and careful listening to one another. Drawing on his years of pastoral experience, Pope Francis again offers helpful advice: "Take time, quality time. This means being ready to listen patiently and attentively to everything the other person wants to say. It requires the self-discipline of not speaking until the time is right. Instead of offering an opinion or advice, we need to be sure that we have heard everything the other person has to say. . . . Often the other spouse does not need a solution to his or her problems, but simply to be heard, to feel that someone has acknowledged their pain, their disappointment, their fear, their anger, their hopes and their dreams" (AL 137).

Besides making time for communication, there are other steps couples can take to sustain intimacy. It is important to prioritize time alone together in the form of weekly date nights or yearly getaways as a couple. These need not be terribly expensive endeavors, but should create space and time for a couple to focus on their relationship. Some couples find it helpful to create ground rules for this time, such as focusing their conversation on things other than their children or their jobs. It is also important for couples to develop shared interests or activities they enjoy doing together. This doesn't mean that couples need to spend all of their time together. It is vital for men and women to have friends other than their spouses. No marriage, no matter how good, can meet all of a person's relational needs. But finding activities to share together is a way to nurture the friendship that is at the heart of marriage.[7] Finally, couples should make it a point to pray together regularly as a couple—both alone and through participation in the Church's liturgical life.

It is possible to envision the function of intimacy in a healthy marriage discussed in this chapter in the form of a flowchart. The differences between men and women color the way they think about, experience, and express intimacy. Sexual intimacy serves to reflect back the spiritual, physical, and verbal/emotional intimacy between the couple and is itself shaped by the virtue of chastity and directed toward the life and love which are the ends of marriage:

Forms of Intimacy in a Healthy Marriage

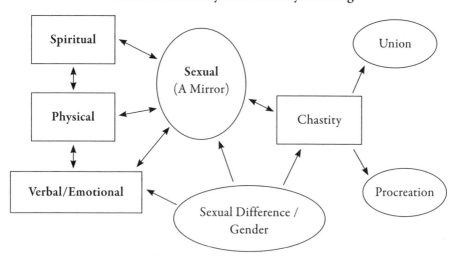

---

7   It is especially important to be wary of time-intensive hobbies that only one spouse pursues because the other does not share the interest—hence the terms "golf widows" or "fishing widows."

THOUGHTS FROM CLAIRE: PRAYING AS A COUPLE AND A FAMILY

Looking back at the thirty-two years of our marriage, I believe that it is the practice of praying as a couple and as a family that has nourished us and sustained us even in times of suffering. Before we got married, both John and I already had a personal relationship with the Lord. We were used to making time each day to pray and to listen to God speak to us through reading Scripture and going to Mass regularly. But once married, we had to learn how to pray and discern together as a couple. This process took time and has changed and evolved over the years.

When it was just the two of us, we continued to pray on our own each day, and then on Sundays we would pray together and also talk about the readings and homily at Mass that day. We would also share with each other what we were learning in our prayer and what we thought God wanted us to be doing. After a while, we began praying together more. We would read and discuss Scripture together in our morning prayer and do night prayer together. When we had a major decision to make, we would pray about it for a while and then discuss what we thought was best. John and I discern in very different ways. He likes to use Ignatian discernment, writing down the pros and cons and then asking God to guide him. I like to take time with the Lord, allowing Him to speak to my heart. We have found that though we pray and discern differently, we usually come to the same solutions. The Holy Spirit speaks to us in different ways.

We have always included the children in some of our prayer. When they were very little, they would join us in morning prayer. John would get out his guitar, and we would sing and praise God together and then read Scripture or stories from the lives of the saints. In evening prayer, we would do an examination of conscience. We would all take turns repenting and asking forgiveness for ways that we had hurt one another. This way the children saw that even Mom and Dad sinned and needed to ask forgiveness—from God and from them. We would also intercede nightly with the kids for family and friends who needed our prayers and always thanked and praised God for answers to our prayers. When we went to adoration, we would often invite them to join us so that they could spend some time with Jesus in the Blessed Sacrament. Praying the Rosary was another priority. We often prayed it together when traveling places in the car.

Life in the Grabowski house was usually very busy. With five children of various ages, our schedule was crazy. It would have been easy to lose sight of our priorities as a family, but with God's grace, we were able to make family prayer the most important part of our week. It was being nourished by the Eucharist and the grace of the other sacraments that enabled us to share our faith with our children. We decided early on that sharing meals—especially dinners—had to be a priority in our lives. This meant that we worked our family schedules to revolve around the Lord's table and the family dinner table. If our kids had sports or practices, we planned around them so that we could attend Saturday evening or Sunday Mass as a family. We also worked at having dinners together—even if it meant waiting until 8:00 p.m. after a sports practice to eat. Dinner was the next most important place we came together to be nourished by good food and conversation. This was the time to share about the joys and struggles of that day. This was the perfect time as parents to catechize our kids. We would spend hours talking about everything from faith, news in the world, our culture, the lives of the saints, philosophy, and even football.

I am grateful that John and I were able to raise our kids in a Christian house where we worked together to pass on our Catholic faith. I am also grateful to see how our grown children are beginning to share their faith with their own children as they marry and start families. Though our children are grown, I see that the priorities we taught our family are still present. When we are all together, we still go to Mass as a family and we still love sharing meals at the dinner table. This is definitely a time to share our many blessings with each other.

We are now pretty much empty-nesters, with our youngest heading off to college in just a few months. We are discovering how praying as a couple can help us make this transition to a new phase of our life together. Because praying together has been a constant in our marriage,

*we are able to support each other as we adjust to this new stage and as
we discern together what God has planned for us next.*

Discussion Questions:

1. How does God view the difference between the sexes (CCC 369)?

2. What does it mean that men and women are complementary to each other (CCC 372)?

3. What vocation are men and women called to share (CCC 373)?

4. How have you seen some of the differences in male and female patterns of communication at work in your relationship with your fiancée or spouse?

5. Why does Pope Francis emphasize the importance of couples spending time together?

6. What are some of the primary obstacles to doing this in our culture?

7. Why is listening essential to effective communication?

8. What steps can you take to foster or deepen habits of effective listening in your relationship?

9. How does our culture understand intimacy (e.g., when two people are said to "be intimate," what does that indicate about their relationship)? What's wrong with this understanding?

10. How would you define intimacy?

11. Have you experienced periods in your relationship when you felt more distant from your fiancée or spouse? What things helped you work through those periods?

12. List seven qualities of conjugal love (CCC 1643).

_____

_____

_____

_____

_____

_____

_____

13. What are the essential properties of marriage (CCC 1644)?

14. What is the basis of family prayer (CCC 2685)?

15. When should Christian couples pray (CCC 2633, 2742, 2745)?

✠ Concluding Prayer ✠

Notes

12

Love for a Lifetime: Conflict Resolution and Investing in Your Marriage

---

OPENING

SCRIPTURE READING:
MATTHEW 25:14–30

SUGGESTED PRAYER:

God, You are the Giver of all gifts. Thank You for the great gifts of love and marriage, which You have created to draw us to Yourself. Help us to treasure the gift of the relationship You have given us. Let us never take this gift for granted but actively work to build it up and deepen it. Let our marriages be a visible sign of Your love to all those around us.

CATECHETICAL REFLECTION

The Parable of the Talents in Matthew's Gospel challenges us to think about our stewardship of God's gifts which He has entrusted to us. In Jesus' day, a "talent" was a unit of measure for something weighty—typically a precious metal like silver or gold. While we can see the significance of this text for the virtue of industriousness in human work (in the United States this is often the Gospel reading on Labor Day), the text is rightly understood more broadly. Our Lord is not exhorting his disciples to become successful venture capitalists. This broader reading is helped by the easy association in our own English idiom of the term "talents" with gifts and abilities. So while the text can rightly be read as calling us to good stewardship of our material possessions, this stewardship extends to all of the gifts given to us by God. For Jesus' hearers, the most "weighty" and precious reality of their lives was the glory of God found within the Temple upon the mercy seat within the Holy of Holies.[1] But whether we take "talents" in a more material or a more spiritual sense, the message is the same: God entrusts gifts to us to be shared and given away, not buried or hoarded out of fear. When we take God's gifts for granted, they dissipate: "For to everyone who has, more will be given and he will grow rich; but from the one who has not, even what he has will be taken away" (Mt 25:29).

As the preceding chapters of this book make clear, Scripture and the Church's Tradition sees marriage as a gift. It is a gift God gives to us in the very act of creation, but is a gift endowed with a new purpose and power in Christ as a sacrament. Jesus Himself binds couples together and gives them the grace to live out their vocation in faithfulness to Him and to one another. But this grace at work in the gift of marriage should not be taken for granted. It is something couples must learn to draw upon, cultivate, and put into action. Two primary ways in which married couples can do this is by developing practices that enable them to work through conflict constructively, and by learning to intentionally invest in their marriage on a daily basis.

As in the case of the original Jewish audience of the parable, the most weighty thing in the lives of the Christian couple is God's presence in their lives, which is the wellspring of mercy for themselves and for one another. Couples can draw upon this mercy and deepen the intimacy in their rela-

---

[1] This is the observation of Bishop Robert Barron. See "The Deeper Meaning of the Parable of the Talents," *The Catholic World Report* (September 22, 2104). http://www.catholicworldreport.com/Blog/3380/the_deeper_meaning_of_the_parable_of_the_talents.aspx.

tionship by learning to work through conflict in non-destructive ways and by giving and receiving forgiveness when conflict does cause hurt. While some couples and even marriage counselors encourage couples to avoid conflict, it is really only destructive forms of conflict that should be avoided. When handled properly, conflict can be a doorway to deeper intimacy and growth in a marriage, enabling couples to continue to bring to the surface and work through expectations or needs that haven't arisen or come to light through other forms of communication.

Many things can cause conflict in a marriage, from triggers in day-to-day life to deeper issues that can emerge or, if ignored, fester over time. Daily triggers for conflict can be things such as misunderstood feelings, stress, tiredness, low blood sugar, or hormonal changes. Deeper issues can be rooted in insecurity, gender or personality differences, unfulfilled expectations, or unmet needs in the relationship. The key is identifying the underlying issue and working through it in a way that builds up rather than damages the marriage.

So what determines the difference between constructive and destructive conflict? Destructive ways of working through conflict include: avoidance of disagreement, passive aggressive forms of expressing displeasure (e.g., the silent treatment), bringing up past arguments or disagreements, resorting to sarcasm or name-calling, making sweeping accusations of the other ("you always" or "you never"), utilizing power statements ("I quit" or "you can sleep on the couch"), or arguing in public or other places that compromise healthy privacy in the relationship. Sometimes these individual practices are part of larger patterns of mishandling conflict that individuals learned within their families of origin or in handling life circumstances over time.

Marriage counselors and psychologists sometimes speak of the "four Fs" in this regard: fight, flight, fold, or fake.[2] The person who opts to

---

[2]　See, for example, John Gray, *Men are from Mars, Women are from Venus: A Practical Guide for Improving Communication and Getting What You Want in Your Relationships* (New York: HarperCollins, 1992), 164–67. Unfortunately, Gray does not distinguish constructive from destructive conflict clearly, giving the impression that all conflict is damaging to a couple's relationship.

make every disagreement a fight will often resort to name-calling, sarcasm, shouting, or other displays of anger. The idea is to get the other person to back down in order to "win" the argument. Conversely, the person who flees conflict simply withdraws at the first sign of disagreement. This withdrawal may be into silence, into another room, or from the house. While this avoids destructive forms of disagreement, this strategy means that underlying issues are never resolved and so the relationship never grows and may actually be undermined over time. The person who folds is the one who always accepts blame for whatever caused the conflict. Like flight, this can smooth things over for a time, but the person who folds is internalizing blame for the marriage's problems, and the relationship does not deepen—indeed the person can become depressed over time. Finally, the attempt to fake one's way out of conflict means that a person never admits to being upset, angry, or disappointed. This is the person who, when asked "what's wrong?" will answer "nothing." This strategy also avoids conflict in the short term but can cause long-term emotional harm as someone "stuffs" important feelings instead of acknowledging them and working through them with a spouse.

These damaging strategies can be employed by either sex, though the first two are more characteristic of men while the second two are more frequently employed by women. In each of these cases, while there may appear to be a winner and a loser or a kind of joint victory through the avoidance of conflict, damage occurs in the relationship, eroding trust, causing emotional harm, or missing an opportunity for growth in understanding and mutual love.

Instead, if couples face disagreement and work through it together, they can often arrive at a "win/win" in which each comes to a deeper understanding of the other's expectations, feelings, or needs. This does not necessarily mean that they compromise or that each person "gets" something he or she sought (though it does not exclude such an outcome). What does such non-destructive conflict resolution look like? In many ways it is the inverse of the destructive practices already described. That is, couples should stick to the immediate issue rather than returning to previous arguments. Husbands and wives should seek to maintain each other's privacy, speak respectfully, and show honor to one another even in the face of real disagreement. It is vital that they seek not just to make their own points but to genuinely listen to the other—both what is being expressed and the feelings that underlie the ideas. Some marriage counselors recommend echoing back the other's thoughts and feelings when working through conflict. Women need to take care to express their feelings directly, lest they confuse their husbands or exacerbate the conflict. Men need to acknowledge their wives' feelings rather than minimizing them or attempting to "fix" them or the situation causing the turmoil.

If tempers flare, spouses can agree to take a break, but they should resume the conversation when they are calmer. If one spouse says something that hurts or offends the other, he or she should ask the other's forgiveness. Again, the advice of the Letter to the Ephesians is an excellent rule of life for a couple: "Be angry but do not sin; do not let the sun set on your anger, and do not leave room for the devil" (Eph 4:26–27). As Pope Francis wisely observes, giving and receiving forgiveness prevents resentment from taking root in our hearts. It also depends upon our own awareness of the mercy we ourselves have received from God:

> All this assumes that we ourselves have had the experience of being forgiven by God, justified by his grace and not by our own merits. We have known a love that is prior to any of our own efforts, a love that constantly opens doors, promotes and encourages. If we accept that God's love is unconditional, that the Father's love cannot be bought or sold, then we will become capable of showing boundless love and forgiving others even if they have wronged us. Otherwise, our family life will no longer be a place of understanding, support and encouragement, but rather one of constant tension and mutual criticism. (AL 108)[3]

The experience of regularly receiving and giving forgiveness is at the heart of growth in marital love and intimacy over time.

---

[3] See the whole analysis of the practice of forgiveness in a family in AL 105–8.

To return for a moment to the financial overtones of the Parable of the Talents, some marriage counselors speak of the importance of "investing in a marriage" or practicing "marital banking" over time. To understand this, think of a marriage as being like a checking account at a bank. Couples are constantly making "withdrawals" and "deposits" in the emotional balance in their relationship, and these impact their closeness to each other.[4] A "deposit" in this scenario would be anything positive or security-producing, something which gives one's spouse energy or affirmation (e.g., physical touch, saying "I love you," spending time together). Conversely, a "withdrawal" would describe anything negative or that causes sadness. One of the important tasks for marital communication is for spouses to come to understand each other's deposits and withdrawals and how these impact their marriage.

Some of the ways people experience love and affirmation is due to gender differences or unique features of their personality, but other aspects are rooted in their childhood and the way they experienced love in their families of origin. One helpful tool to help couples unlock their own and their spouse's preferred "deposits" is the concept of "love languages." Gary Chapman speaks of five basic love languages through which people experience love: words of affirmation, physical touch, acts of service, gifts, and quality time.[5] According to Chapman, every person has a primary and a secondary love language, learned over the course of their lives. People tend to favor their own preferred love languages as ways to express love, but this may not be effective at building up the emotional bank account in the relationship if one's spouse speaks different love languages. It requires time, observation, and honest communication for spouses to come to learn to speak each other's love languages successfully.

---

[4] See, for example Greg and Lisa Popcak, *For Better and Forever: A Catholic Guide to Lifelong Marriage*, revised and expanded edition (Huntington, IN: Our Sunday Visitor, 2016), chap. 10; Greg and Lisa Popcak, *Discovering God Together: The Catholic Guide to Raising Faithful Kids*, (Manchester, NH: Sophia Institute Press, 2015), 19–20.

[5] See Gary Chapman, *The Five Love Languages: The Secret to Love that Lasts* (Chicago: Northfield Publishing, 1992). Several editions of this bestselling book have been published over the years, including the most recent one in 2015.

Nonetheless, it is possible to identify some common withdrawals and deposits for both sexes. Women frequently mention things like being ignored, their husbands "never" being on time, or their husbands spending too much time away from home (hence the term "golf widows" or "fishing widows"). Men frequently mention nagging (which they hear as criticism of their competence) or their wives never initiating sex. Either sex might complain about feeling controlled by the other. On the positive side of the ledger, common deposits for women include: daily expressions of love, praise (both for her and for their kids), husbands making time for daily communication, playing with children, or shopping together. When asked about their deposits, men often mention things like non-directive encouragement from their wives, or their wives taking the initiative sexually. In general, couples need a five-to-one balance of deposits to withdrawals to maintain a positive emotional balance sheet necessary for a healthy, loving relationship.[6]

Working through conflict in non-destructive ways and seeking daily to maintain a strong and healthy emotional balance sheet in a marriage requires work—sometimes hard work. But it is worth recalling that developing habits of this kind is a response to and is made possible by the grace given through the sacraments and sustained in the life of the Church. The love that grows and flourishes in the Sacrament of Marriage is watered by mutual forgiveness and nurtured by daily decisions to invest time, affirmation, and energy in one's spouse. In this way, the precious gift of marriage entrusted to the couple can flourish and increase, and like the prudent servants in the Parable of the Talents, the couple can hear their Master's affirmation: "Well done, my good and faithful servant[s]. Since you were faithful in small matters, I will give you great responsibilities. Come, share your master's joy" (Mt 25:21).

To revisit the flowchart that introduced the way in which intimacy should function in a healthy marriage, in light of this further discussion we might make the following additions:

---

[6] For these gender-specific withdrawals and deposits and the 5:1 ratio, see Gary Smalley, *Making Love Last Forever* (Dallas: Word Publishing, 1996), 251–64.

Forms of Intimacy in a Healthy Marriage

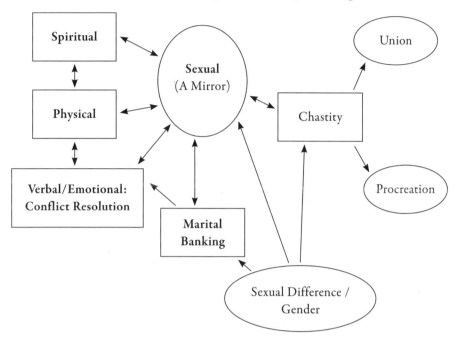

THOUGHTS FROM CLAIRE: INVESTING IN YOUR MARRIAGE AND LOVE LANGUAGES

Investing in your marriage is definitely something that every couple needs to consider and make a priority if they want their marriage to grow over their life together. John and I have tried hard to take time for us as a couple at every phase of our marriage. This can get a lot harder when you begin having children and your busy lives as a couple get even busier. Remembering date nights was an important practice for us, even if it meant just spending a few hours together after we put the kids to bed. We have always been on a tight budget, so most of the time we tried to be creative in doing things that didn't cost any money. We love to play games together, so as long as we could keep our competitive natures in check, we would spend time playing cards or tennis together. I can remember going to a park with a playground next to the tennis courts so we could play while still keeping an eye on our four little kids.

We have also tried hard to get away together without the kids, even if it was only for a night, at least once a year. Once after doing marriage preparation with a couple, they offered to watch our children for a weekend to thank us. This was one of the best gifts they could have given us. I think that getting away together is not only good for the parents, but the children can benefit as well. At first, our almost eight-year-old daughter Bekah wasn't happy that we were going away without her and asked why she and her siblings couldn't come with us. I simply explained to her that when Mom and Dad go away and get some rest, they are better parents when they get home. I think that must have been the Holy Spirit's inspiration because our eight-year-old understood that she wanted her Mom and Dad to come home and be more patient and peaceful. I truly believe that when a couple's relationship is strong and loving, they are better able to show love to their children.

John and I have different love languages. He is definitely an "acts of service-" type guy, while I much prefer quality time together. The greatest gift anyone can give me is their time and attention. My fortieth birthday fell on a Saturday in the summer, and all I wanted was to spend a day with John and the kids hiking and having a picnic in the park. I didn't know that John had planned a surprise party for me at our house that night. I was disappointed and upset when he told me that he couldn't come to the park with us because he had things to do. He said that I would understand later. But I didn't want to understand later; I wanted him to be with me and the kids enjoying a beautiful day outside. He had already planned the party and needed to spend the day getting ready. While it was nice to see my friends that night at the party, I must admit that I don't have fond memories of my birthday that year. All I really wanted was John's presence, but he wanted to do something for me. From this and other experiences, we have learned that just because we receive love in certain ways, we can't simply use our own love language to show love. It is so important to understand how our spouse receives love and to express it in that way.

As I look back on our marriage, I am grateful that we have taken time to work on our relationship. I do believe that I married my best friend; now as our children are leaving home and beginning their own lives and families, I still have my best friend around to support me. It isn't always easy adjusting to a new phase of life and learning to let go of children, but it sure is easier when you have someone accompanying you. I am grateful that we can lean on each other in seeking God's will for our life as a couple. We have shared many joys and sorrows over the years and have much to look forward to together. We've seen the modest efforts we've made to work at our marriage over the years richly blessed by God's mercy and generosity.

Discussion Questions:

1. How is our dignity as persons connected to our freedom (CCC 1730)?

2. How does our freedom reach its perfection (CCC 1731)?

3. What does the Church understand by "participation" and how might it relate to marriage (CCC 1913)?

4. Why is repeated forgiveness a sign of the couple's and family's role as a domestic church (CCC 1657)?

5. In the Christian family, whose responsibility is it to grant forgiveness (CCC 2227)?

6. What are some negative strategies for resolving conflict that were part of your family of origin?

7. What are some healthy strategies for resolving conflict that were part of your family of origin?

8. Describe your first (or most recent) disagreement as a couple. What caused it? What negative strategies for resolving conflict did you employ? What positive or healthy strategies did you use?

9. Describe a time when you achieved a "win/win" in working through a disagreement with each other (i.e., came to a deeper knowledge of one another's needs and expectations even if you didn't get exactly what you wanted)? What made the difference in getting to that outcome?

10. What overall patterns in handling conflict in your relationship would you like to build on?

11. What overall patterns in dealing with conflict in your relationship would you like to change?

12. What would you say are your two primary love languages? What are those of your spouse or fiancée? Compare answers with each other.

13. List seven things your spouse/fiancée did for you in the past week that you experienced as a "deposit":

_____

_____

_____

_____

_____

_____

_____

14. List six things your spouse/fiancée did in the past week that you experienced as a "withdrawal":

_____

_____

_____

_____

_____

_____

15. Do your answers to the previous two questions shed any further light on question 10 above?

16. Compose a prayer of affirmation and blessing for your fiancée/spouse, thanking God for his or her gifts and asking God to use them to build up your family and His Kingdom.

✠ Concluding Prayer ✠

Notes

13

CONCLUSION

Marriage Formation: A Beginning—Not an End

·

The Church is in the midst of a fundamental shift in the way She forms marriages. Some thirty-five years ago; Saint John Paul II expanded our vision of marriage preparation to include a process of formation that began in childhood and culminated in the intense period of immediate preparation prior to the wedding. But John Paul II hinted at the need to extend this process of formation beyond the wedding. He stated: "In order that the family may be ever more a true community of love, it is necessary that all its members should be helped and trained in their responsibilities as they face the new problems that arise, in mutual service, and in active sharing in family life. This holds true especially for young families, which, finding themselves in a context of new values and responsibilities, are more vulnerable, especially in the first years of marriage, to possible difficulties, such as those created by adaptation to life together or by the birth of children" (FC 69). In other words, marriage formation is more than just what happens "pre-Cana"; it must continue into marriage.

Pope Francis has expanded this call for ongoing formation and accompaniment of couples beyond the wedding. This is especially true for the newly married. As he noted in *Amoris laetitia*: "... it is all the more essential that couples be helped during the first years of their married life to enrich and deepen their conscious and free decision to have, hold and love one another for life. Often the engagement period is not long enough, the decision is precipitated for various reasons and, what is even more problematic, the couple themselves are insufficiently mature. As a result, the newly married couple need to complete a process that should have taken place during their engagement" (AL 217).[1] Marriage formation must continue beyond the wedding so that couples can continue to grow in their understanding and ability to live out the sacrament they have received.

What should such ongoing formation look like? As a Church we are still at the initial stages of articulating an answer. In addition to our years of preparing engaged couples for marriage, this book is the fruit of eight years of experience of being part of a post-Cana marriage ministry at the parish level. Our initial efforts in that ministry took the form of planning event-based monthly meetings for couples in our parish. The formats of these events varied from "theology on tap" presentations to movie nights with discussion to romantic dinners for couples around Valentine's Day. We aimed to provide already married couples with opportunities for "fun, faith formation, fellowship, and (usually) food." The response to these events varied greatly. Some nights we had overwhelming turnout while on other evenings we saw very minimal participation. But in neither case did we see ongoing fruit in the form of deeper relationships among couples.

A few years ago after more prayer and discernment, we moved in a new direction. We started offering formation courses over twelve weeks. The format of the evening was a talk focused on some aspect of marriage as disclosed in Scripture or the teaching of the Church. This was followed by a witness from a couple who presented their own experience of the reality discussed (both blessings and challenges), and then sharing in small groups.[2] The change brought fruit that we had not seen before.

---

[1] Note that "post-Cana" accompaniment is the theme of §§217–30 of the document.
[2] The format is not original. It is very similar used to that of the ChristLife series used in many Catholic parishes: Discovering Christ, Following Christ, and Sharing Christ. For more information see "ChristLife Series," ChristLife Catholic Ministry for Evangelization, accessed February 20, 2017, https://christlife.org/christlife-series.

Our ministry team began to grow. The first year we offered the course we had twenty couples take part. The second year we had twice that many (including a number of couples who had gone through the previous year). We also saw much deeper and more supportive relationships begin to form among these couples. We had everything from engaged couples to couples who had been married fifty-plus years—and all of them benefitted in different ways from the experience. For the engaged or newly married, it was a deeper immersion in the Church's vision than they had experienced in their pre-Cana programs. For those married for some time, the experience was more like a form of mystagogical catechesis—an unpacking of the sacrament that they had celebrated and were already living. The older couples also found that they had a wealth of experience and wisdom to share even as they received a deeper sense of the Church's vision and language to describe what they somehow already knew and were living.

Seeing this dynamic at work confirmed what we had discovered in our twenty-five years of working with couples in marriage preparation: the act of teaching and sharing our own experience with other couples invariably strengthens and builds up our own marriage. The famous axiom often attributed to St. Francis that "it is in giving that we receive" has been verified over and over in our own experience as well as in that of others who are part of this ministry. This book could be used in such a course. But the information will only benefit couples who are actually willing to do the work of reading, prayerful study, reflection, and discussion. It will be more beneficial still to those who undertake this study with other couples either in a couple-to-couple format or in groups. Married couples need such friends beyond their spouse. As we stated previously, no relationship—no matter how good—can meet all of a person's needs for friendship and communion with others. This is especially true for Christians who, as members of the body of Christ, are also members of one another. Christian marriage flourishes in community with others.

In *Familiaris consortio*, Saint John Paul II compared the process of marriage formation to the catechumenate by which one enters the Church as an adult (most commonly known as RCIA) (see FC 66). Once again, Pope Francis has echoed and expanded on these ideas of his predecessor. In a recent address, the Holy Father called for a new marriage catechumenate: "In this spirit, I would like to stress the need for a 'new catechumenate' for marriage preparation. Welcoming the support of the Fathers of the last Ordinary Synod, it is urgent to effectively implement what has already been proposed in *Familiaris Consortio* (n. 66). Namely, just as the catechumenate is part of the sacramental process for the baptism of adults, so too may the preparation for marriage form an integral part of the whole sacramental procedure of marriage, as an antidote to prevent the increase of invalid or inconsistent marriage celebrations."[3] The celebration of the wedding, though an important milestone for a couple, is not an end—it is a beginning. Like the sacraments of initiation, the wedding merely marks a deeper mode of incorporation into the ongoing life and mission of the Church.

Following the teaching of the Second Vatican Council, both Saint John Paul II and Pope Francis have described the Christian family as a "domestic church." This means that it shares in the offices of Christ as priest, king, and prophet (see LG 11; FC 50; AL 67). The priesthood of the couple (in the understanding of the Western Latin Church) begins at the wedding when the couple confer the Sacrament of Marriage on each other. In the priestly office, the couple and their family share in the Church's life as a worshipping community through prayer together in their household and their participation in the liturgy of the Church. The Eucharist is the "source and summit" of this life of prayer—everything in the family's spiritual life flows from it and all of their work, love, and prayer culminates in their offering of themselves in the Eucharist (see FC 57; LG 11; AL 318).

Kingship in Christian circles has always been understood in terms of service after the example of Jesus who came not to be served but to serve and to give His life for our salvation (see Mk 10:45). The Ortho-

---

3   Pope Francis, "Address of His Holiness Pope Francis to the Officials of the Tribunal of the Roman Rota for the Inauguration of the Judicial Year," January 21, 2017, http://w2.vatican.va/content/francesco/en/speeches/2017/january/documents/papa-francesco_20170121_anno-giudiziario-rota-romana.html.

dox Churches remind couples of this kingly dignity restored to us in Christ by placing crowns on the heads of couples in the celebration of the wedding liturgy. This royal dignity of the spouses is conveyed in and through all of the myriad expressions of daily life, work, service, reconciliation, and self-gift that are the fabric of a family's daily life. The bread and the wine of the Eucharistic gifts can be understood as symbolizing the work, substance, and joys of a family's life, which we offer on the altar and are transformed into the presence of Christ in their midst.

Finally, a Christian couple and their family are prophetic by simply living their vocation. Indeed, the choice to get married is itself a prophetic act in a culture that increasingly avoids or trivializes marriage. This prophetic witness is underscored by couples who choose to marry in the Church and to try to celebrate their weddings simply, resisting the pressures of social custom and the wedding industry.[4] The choice to have a simple wedding can help couples embark on their life together in an effort to promote justice and strive for simplicity of life in the midst of a consumer culture, and then to pass on these same values to the children that they welcome into their family. But these deeds must also be matched by words. The Christian couple and their family is meant to be both an evangelized and an evangelizing community—hearing the word of God proclaimed by the Church and then speaking that same word in their home and community (see FC 54).

Lay people and families have a unique role in the New Evangelization. As Pope Francis tells us: "The new evangelization calls for personal involvement on the part of each and every one of the baptized. Every Christian is challenged, here and now, to be actively engaged in evangelization" (EG 120). The reason for the Church's recent focus on the family in the Synods of 2014 and 2015 was precisely to highlight the way in which married couples and families are meant to be at the forefront of the Church's evangelizing effort: "The Synod Fathers emphasized that Christian families, by the grace of the sacrament of matrimony, are the principal agents of the family apostolate, above all through 'their joy-

---

[4] Pope Francis makes this point about simple weddings in *Amoris laetitia*, §212.

filled witness as domestic churches.' . . . It is not enough to show generic concern for the family in pastoral planning. Enabling families to take up their role as active agents of the family apostolate calls for 'an effort at evangelization and catechesis inside the family'" (AL 200). Marriage formation before and after the wedding is meant to equip couples to respond to this call to evangelization.

Hopefully, working through this text with your spouse has begun this process of providing deeper formation in the vision that Scripture and the Church teaching offers. Of course, there is always more to learn—about this vision, about what it means to live it out, and about what it means to love your spouse! Just as investing in your marriage is meant to become an ongoing habit, trying to understand and live this great sacrament more fully is an ongoing endeavor for couples made fruitful by the grace God continually offers to us.

One does not have to be an expert in evangelization before beginning to evangelize. Pope Francis puts the matter well and leaves us with our concluding challenge:

Every Christian is a missionary to the extent that he or she has encountered the love of God in Christ Jesus: we no longer say that we are "disciples" and "missionaries," but rather that we are always "missionary disciples." If we are not convinced, let us look at those first disciples, who, immediately after encountering the gaze of Jesus, went forth to proclaim him joyfully: "We have found the Messiah!" (*Jn* 1:41). The Samaritan woman became a missionary immediately after speaking with Jesus and many Samaritans [. . . came] to believe in him "because of the woman's testimony" (*Jn* 4:39). So too, Saint Paul, after his encounter with Jesus Christ, "immediately proclaimed Jesus" (*Acts* 9:20; cf. 22:6–21). So what are we waiting for? (EG 120)

Indeed, as couples and families who are living cells of the Body of Christ, what are we waiting for?

14

APPENDICES

Special Topics and Further Resources

A. WEDDINGS: SIMPLE IS BEAUTIFUL

A survey commissioned by the popular wedding planning website The Knot found that the average cost of a wedding in the United States in 2016 had risen to $35,329—significantly more in many urban areas.[1] What is supposed to be a visible and liturgical proclamation of the Gospel message of Christ giving His life for His bridal Church reflected in the love of the couple can easily become instead a display of wealth, social status, or political connection. Family expectations and the pressures of the wedding industry to make the day "perfect" can overwhelm a couple's resolve to try to keep things simple. Conversely, for poorer couples the pageantry and expense of weddings can discourage them from marrying altogether. Pope Francis articulates a very direct challenge to engaged couples and those helping them to prepare for their weddings: "Here let me say a word to fiancés. Have the courage to be different. Don't let yourselves get swallowed up by a society of consumption and empty appearances. What is important is the love you share, strengthened and sanctified by grace. You are capable of opting for a more modest and simple celebration in which love takes precedence over everything else.

---

[1]   Maggie Seaver, "The National Average Cost of a Wedding Hits $35,329," The Knot, https://www.theknot.com/content/average-wedding-cost-2016.

Pastoral workers and the entire community can help make this priority the norm rather than the exception" (AL 212).

There are many resources with tips for planning simple Catholic weddings. Some particularly helpful sources of information are noted here.

Resources

Calis, Stephanie. *Invited: The Ultimate Catholic Wedding Planner.* Boston: Pauline, 2016.
Checklist and print resources.

Catechism of the Catholic Church, 1621–37.

Catholic Wedding Help. "Planning your Catholic wedding: A checklist." http://catholicweddinghelp.com/wedding-planning/wedding-planning.htm.
Checklist and print resources.

USCCB. "Wedding Ceremony." http://www.usccb.org/issues-and-action/marriage-and-family/marriage/wedding-ceremony/.
Article with resources and links.

B. COHABITATION: WHY NOT?

Unfortunately, the practice of cohabitation before marriage has become the norm in many parts of the world. Some of the biblical and theological reasons why the Church opposes the practice should be clear from this book—especially chapter 7. As Saint John Paul II taught: "The total physical self-giving [of sexual intercourse] would be a lie if it were not the sign and fruit of a total personal self-giving, in which the whole person, including the temporal dimension, is present: if the person were to withhold something or reserve the possibility of deciding otherwise in the future, by this very fact he or she would not be giving totally" (FC 11). Pope Francis wisely notes that this teaching holds true even for engaged couples: "The Church, in her wisdom, guards the *distinction between being engaged and being spouses*—it's not the same—especially in view of the delicateness and depth of this test. . . . The powerful symbols of the body hold the keys to the soul: We cannot treat the bonds of the flesh lightly, without opening some lasting wound in the spirit (see 1 Cor 6:15–20)."[2]

While many social scientists in the 1960's and 70's put forward the opinion that the practice of cohabitation might reduce the incidence of divorce by enabling people to see whether they are compatible—sexually and otherwise, more recent research dispels this idea. Many cohabiting couples never marry. Those who do are at a significantly greater risk for later marital failure than those who don't. Why? Those who have studied the issue point to a number of factors.[3] First, couples who cohabit before marriage often have the view that if something goes wrong, they can simply "move out." Those who later marry carry the same "open door mentality" into the marriage, making it more likely that they will leave rather than work through problems together. Second, couples who cohabit often try to avoid conflict rather than resolve it, causing the relationship to fail to grow and deepen over time in the way described in chapter 12. Third, we know that sex creates powerful biochemical bonds between persons.

---

[2] Pope Francis, General Audience, May 27, 2015, http://w2.vatican.va/content/francesco/en/audiences/2015/documents/papa-francesco_20150527_udienza-generale.html.

[3] These ideas are somewhat commonplace in literature which reviews social scientific data on cohabitation. On these and other negative effects of cohabitation, see the USCCB statement "Marriage Preparation and Cohabiting Couples" (1999). http://www.usccb.org/issues-and-action/marriage-and-family/marriage/marriage-preparation/cohabiting.cfm; see also Linda Waite and Maggie Gallagher, *The Case for Marriage: Why Married People Are Happier, Healthier, and Better Off Financially* (New York: Broadway Books, 2000), 36–46. While the studies cited in these sources are a bit dated, more recent research supports most of their findings. See the entry on "Cohabitation" on the For Your Marriage website of the USCCB: http://www.foryourmarriage.org/catholic-marriage/church-teachings/cohabitation/. See also the excellent essay by Cassandra Hough, "The Fullness of Sexuality: Church Teaching on Premarital Sex," in *Women, Sex, and the Church: A Case for Catholic Teaching*, Erika Bachiochi, ed., (Boston: Pauline, 2012), 57-78. Hough effectively blends Church teaching and social scientific data in making her case.

Couples who are engaging in sex with a person while trying to determine if he or she is a good potential spouse are putting on biochemical blinders that can cause them to miss important clues that this person is not a good match. Given how painful and destructive divorce can be, it is much better to come to this realization before the marriage than after (see AL 209).

Resources

Catechism of the Catholic Church, 2353, 2390–91.

Hough, Cassandra. "The Fullness of Sexuality: Church Teaching on Pre-marital Sex." In *Women, Sex, and the Church: A Case for Catholic Teaching*, Ericha Bachiochi, ed., 57–78. Boston: Pauline, 2012.

USCCB. "Cohabitation." For Your Marriage. http://www.foryourmarriage.org/catholic-marriage/church-teachings/cohabitation/. *Article with resources and links.*

USCCB. "Marriage Preparation and Cohabiting Couples." 1999. http://www.usccb.org/issues-and-action/marriage-and-family/marriage/marriage-preparation/cohabiting.cfm.

C. THE GIFT OF CHILDREN, RESPONSIBLE PARENTHOOD, DEALING WITH INFERTILITY

Once past puberty, healthy men and women have very different patterns of fertility. In general, men are always fertile, though their fertility typically declines with age or can be lost through illness or accident. Women, on the other hand, have a definite window of fertile years between the onset of menstruation and menopause and are fertile only for a few days in a given menstrual cycle.

As described above in chapter 7, the Church teaches that methods of fertility awareness (NFP) can be used to enable couples to postpone pregnancy when there are serious reasons to avoid welcoming children for a period of time. What many people do not realize is that these same methods can help couples become pregnant, even if their fertility is limited in some way.

Infertility affects both men and women. Infertility is not itself a disease, but a symptom of an underlying disease impacting the body's normal function. Fertility can also be hindered by lifestyle issues such as obesity, smoking, and number of sexual partners.[4] Infertility can place an enormous strain on marriage and the Church recognizes it as a cross in the lives of the many couples who experience it (CCC 2379).

Methods of fertility awareness or natural family planning, especially coupled with medical intervention aimed at treating the disease of which infertility is a symptom (NaPro technology),[5] can restore some persons to health and aid couples with limited fertility to conceive and bear children. In cases where the couple is genuinely infertile, the Church recommends the practice of adoption as another way to realize the fruitfulness of their mutual love. As Pope Francis observes: "Adopting a child is an act of love, offering the gift of a family to someone who has none. It is important to insist that legislation help facilitate the adoption process, above all in the case of unwanted children, in order to prevent their abortion or abandonment. Those who accept the challenge of adopting and accepting someone unconditionally and gratuitously become channels of God's love" (AL 179). Adoptive parents make a covenant with the child they welcome into their family and, as we saw in chapter 5, in the perspective of Scripture, this covenant creates a bond as real as a blood relation.

---

[4] On these and other causes of infertility, see Katie Elrod and Paul Carpentier, "The Church's Best Kept Secret: Church Teaching on Infertility Treatment," in Erika Bachiochi, ed., *Women, Sex, and Church: A Case for Catholic Teaching* (Boston: Pauline, 2010), 122–25.

[5] NaPro Technology uses a combination of targeted medical intervention (e.g., microsurgery, low doses of hormones, and/or fertility drugs) aimed at treating the underlying disease of which fertility is the symptom. It joins this medical treatment with the Creighton Model of Fertility Awareness (a method of NFP) to help couples achieve pregnancy by restoring the body's fertility. See the excellent overview of this approach provided by Elrod and Carpentier, "The Church's Best Kept Secret," 121–40, and how it coheres with the Church's vision.

Resources

Catechism of the Catholic Church. "Adoption," 2379; "Natural Forms of Birth Regulation," 2366–72; "Infertility," 2373–79.

Couple to Couple League. https://ccli.org/.
Details on the symptom-thermal methods of fertility awareness.

The Creighton Model Fertility Care System. http://www.creighton-model.com/.
Details on the Creighton model of the Billings method and NaPro Technology resources.

Elrod, Katie and Paul Carpentier. "The Church's Best Kept Secret: Church Teaching on Infertility Treatment." In *Women, Sex, and the Church: A Case for Catholic Teaching.* Edited by Ericha Bachiochi. Boston: Pauline, 2012.

Marquette Model of NFP. http://www.marquette.edu/nursing/natural-family-planning/model.shtml.
This method uses the Clearblue Easy Fertility Monitor.

Santamaria, Carmen and Angelique Ruhi-Lopez. *The Infertility Companion for Catholics: Spiritual and Practical Support for Couples.* Notre Dame, IN: Ave Maria Press, 2012.

USCCB. "Natural Family Planning" http://www.usccb.org/issues-and-action/marriage-and-family/natural-family-planning/.
Article with links and resources.

D. MANAGING MONEY TOGETHER

In 2014 the American Psychological Association reported results of its survey on stress in America. The study found that disagreement over money was a major source of conflict for almost one third of all couples (31%). Other research supports this finding.[6]

This conflict can have different causes. It can come from different attitudes, priorities, or ways of handling money in the couple's families of origin. It can come from differing expectations and assumptions about money and spending that couples have not brought up and worked through together. Or it can come from the stress produced by the sense that couples cannot direct and plan the way their money is spent—rather it simply "happens to them."

Both Scripture and the Church's teaching have much to say about the right use of money. The Tenth Commandment warns us against covetous desire for the money and possessions of others (see Ex 20:17; Deut 5:21). Jesus challenges us to poverty of heart (see Mt 5:3) and to resist having "two masters"—God and mammon (see Mt 6:24). The sixteenth-century Roman Catechism, which followed the Council of Trent, puts it well: "He who loves money never has money enough."[7] Followers of Jesus are called to strive for simplicity of life, to use their resources for the building up of the Kingdom of God, and to assist their brothers and sisters who have less than they do. This can be a challenge for Christians even of fairly modest means who are bombarded by the contrary messages of a consumer culture which valorizes excess as "luxury" or status, and views people as disposable (see EG 53–56).

Given that good stewardship of money is a key to marital harmony as well as to being a faithful follower of Jesus, it is vital that couples work to get on the same page regarding their money. This means limiting their spending in order to live simply, working to pay off debt, prudently saving in order to be able to deal with health challenges and retirement,

---

[6] See "Happy Couples: How to Avoid Money Arguments," American Psychological Association, http://www.apa.org/helpcenter/money-conflict.aspx.

[7] *Roman Catechism*, III, 37, cited in CCC 2536.

and giving generously in support of the Church and important charitable causes. Some Catholic parishes have found it beneficial to offer programs developed by Evangelical Christian talk show hosts and financial advisors such as Dave Ramsey or Larry Burkett insofar as they encourage many of these aims. However, there are other good financial teachers and programs available. The key is for couples to agree on their priorities in light of their faith and to learn to work together to achieve them.

Resources

Catechism of the Catholic Church, 2534–57.

Crown Financial Ministries. http://www.crown.org/.
Books and programs developed by Larry Burkett.

Lenahan, Phil. *7 Steps to Becoming Financially Free: A Catholic Guide to Managing Your Money.* Huntington, IN: Our Sunday Visitor, 2006. *A book and workbook.*

Ramsey Solutions. www.daveramsey.com.
Books and programs developed by Dave Ramsey.

USCCB. For Your Marriage. www.foryourmarriage.org.
This website has a variety of practical resources related to money. See, for example: http://www.foryourmarriage.org/everymarriage/ overcoming-obstacles/finances.

E. THE POISON OF PORNOGRAPHY

One of the joint effects of the Sexual Revolution and the rapid expansion of technology in recent decades has been the explosion of pornography throughout our culture. What had been an unseemly product only found in seedy parts of town in the mid-twentieth century gradually expanded into neighborhood drug and grocery stores. The video boom of the 1980's made pornographic movies widely available in local video stores and more common in people's homes. The development of the internet, and the expansion of ways to access it, has put pornographic material just clicks away on millions of devices in millions of households. The average age of first exposure to pornography by children in American families is now eight years old.[8]

As technology made pornography more accessible, the Sexual Revolution has promoted it as harmless "adult" entertainment or material which enhances a couple's sexual relationship. Nothing could be further from the truth. Pornography warps users' views of themselves and others, causing them to view themselves and others as objects rather than as persons made in the image and likeness of God. Young people growing up in a pornified culture routinely objectify others as "porn-worthy" or not. Pornography is highly addictive and its use is one of the basic building blocks of the growing phenomenon of sexual addiction.[9]

It also destroys marriages and families. Far from enhancing sexual intimacy in a couple's relationship, pornography consumption conditions people to dissociate sexual sensation from emotional connection to another person, leaving them increasingly isolated. Married people who become ensnared in pornography consumption often withdraw emotionally and physically from their spouses. It is easier to escape into a fantasy with a virtual image than to do the hard work of building and maintaining intimacy with a real flesh and blood person. But, because real sexual intimacy is only a mirror of the other forms of intimacy in a marriage, pornography cannot deliver what it promises. Devoid of real connection with another in love, the porn user is left like Narcissus, staring at an empty image of him- or herself, increasingly enslaved to compulsions that he or she cannot control.

---

[8] See Rob Jackson, "When Children View Pornography," Focus on the Family, http:// www.focusonthefamily.com/parenting/sexuality/when-children-use-pornography/ when-children-view-pornography.

[9] Other building blocks include sexual fantasy and compulsive masturbation. See Mark Laaser, *Healing the Wounds of Sexual Addiction* (Grand Rapids, MI: Zondervan, 2004), 28–35.

When people find themselves struggling with compulsive pornography use, they often need the assistance of others to break these vicious habits. Pastors, therapists, support groups, and online accountability software can help a person break free of pornography and seek healing from its damaging effects. The resources below offer a deeper understanding of the problem, as well as resources available to people seeking to gain freedom from pornography use. The good news is that it is possible for persons and couples to recover from the damage inflicted by pornography consumption and addiction, especially with God's healing grace and the support of others.

Resources

Bransfield, J. Brian. *Overcoming Pornography Addiction: A Spiritual Solution*. New York: Paulist, 2013.

Catechism of the Catholic Church, 2354.

Eberstadt, Mary. *Adam and Eve after the Pill: Paradoxes of the Sexual Revolution*. San Francisco: Ignatius, 2012.

Fradd, Matt. *Delivered: True Stories of Men and Women Who Turned from Porn to Purity*. El Cajon, CA: Catholic Answers Press, 2014.

Kleponis, Peter. *Integrity Restored: Helping Catholic Families Win the Battle Against Pornography*. Steubenville, OH: Emmaus Road, 2014.

LeJeune, Marcel. *Cleansed: A Catholic Guide to Freedom from Porn*. Boston: Pauline, 2016.

Struthers, William. *Wired for Intimacy: How Pornography Hijacks the Male Brain*. Downers Grove, IL: IVP Books, 2010.

USCCB. *Create in Me a Clean Heart: A Pastoral Response to Pornography*. 2015. http://www.usccb.org/issues-and-action/human-life-and-dignity/pornography/upload/Create-in-Me-a-Clean-Heart-Statement-on-Pornography.pdf.

F. ASKING FOR HELP: ADDICTIONS AND ABUSE

Addiction in marriage can take forms besides compulsive pornography consumption or different forms of sexual addiction. Alcoholism, addiction to other drugs, or further destructive behaviors such as habitual gambling or various eating disorders can wreak havoc on previously happy lives and relationships. When these horrors manifest themselves in a couple's life, it is time for them to seek help outside of the walls of their home. Here again, pastors, counselors, therapists, and twelve-step recovery programs can offer help both to the person struggling with the addiction and to the spouse and children seeking to understand and assist him or her on the path of recovery without enabling further destructive behavior. Understanding family and friends can also offer assistance and encouragement during the journey of recovery and rebuilding relationships. While addiction is a disease of isolation, it should not be faced alone by a couple or a family.

Another situation that requires outside help for a couple is the scourge of domestic violence. The U.S. bishops have noted that such violence can take "physical, sexual, psychological, or verbal" forms. While such violence is most often directed at women, men can also be its victims.[10] Pope Francis has decried violence against women by men in their homes as "craven acts of cowardice" (AL 54) and stated that: "In some cases, respect for one's own dignity and the good of the children requires not giving in to excessive demands or preventing a grave injustice, violence or chronic ill-treatment. In such cases, 'separation becomes inevitable. At times it

---

[10] USCCB, "When I Call for Help: A Pastoral response to Domestic Violence against Women," revised ed. (2002).

even becomes morally necessary, precisely when it is a matter of removing the more vulnerable spouse or young children from serious injury due to abuse and violence, from humiliation and exploitation, and from disregard and indifference'. Even so, 'separation must be considered as a last resort, after all other reasonable attempts at reconciliation have proved vain'" (AL 241).

While separation or civil divorce do not break the bond of marriage in the Church's understanding, they can be necessary steps to protect oneself or one's children from further harm in a situation of abuse.

Resources

Alcoholics Anonymous. http://www.aa.org/.
Information about recovery from alcoholism with program literature and connections to local groups.

Catholics for Family Peace. http://www.catholicsforfamilypeace.org/.
Information about and resources to help overcome domestic violence.

Gamblers Anonymous. https://www.gamblersanonymous.org/.
Information about recovery from compulsive gambling with program literature and connections to local groups.

Narcotics Anonymous. https://www.na.org/.
Information about recovery from other drugs with program literature and connections to local groups.

Overeaters Anonymous. https://oa.org/.
Information about recovery from eating disorders with program literature and connections to local groups.

USCCB. "When I Call for Help: A Pastoral response to Domestic Violence against Women." Revised edition. 2002. http://www.usccb.org/issues-and-action/marriage-and-family/marriage/domestic-violence/when-i-call-for-help.cfm.

G. THE SEASONS OF MARRIAGE:
LOVE FOR A LIFETIME

As the final chapters of this book make clear, marriage takes ongoing work on the part of a couple. Couples in good marriages who love each other, pray together, communicate, and work through conflict together still go through stages in which they feel closer or more distant from each other. No marriage is immune to the suffering that life brings. It is not for nothing that couples promise in their vows to be faithful in good times and bad, in sickness and in health.

The good news for Christian couples is that they have more than their own strength to face these challenges. The grace of God, which binds them together in the sacrament, gives them the power to love, to forgive, and to serve when their own resources fail. Christ walks with them in the journey of marriage, and the living water of the Holy Spirit flows from their hearts (see Jn 4:14) and is ever renewed in the sacraments they receive in the life of the Church. As the Body of Christ, the Church offers a wealth of resources to assist couples on their journey together. There are many programs aimed at strengthening good marriages and helping couples navigate through the stages of marriage together. There are also resources that can help to repair and rebuild marriages that have been damaged or wounded in some way. Parishes and Christian communities also offer the invaluable resource of other couples and families seeking to live out their vocation of love and holiness more fully.

Resources

Annunciation Ministries. http://www.annunciationministries.com/.
Marriage resources for couples, parishes, and dioceses.

Giblin, Paul. "Stages of Growth in Marriage." Available on the USCCB's
For Your Marriage website: http://www.foryourmarriage.org/stages-
of-marriage/.

Heap, Laurie. *THRIVE! Together for Life.* Center of Relationships, LLC,
2017.
*More information about this program and more resources from Dr.
Heap can be found at http://ruhealthyruhappymd.com/thrive-2/
sub-page1/#.WNE6bPnyu70.*

Holbock, Ferdinand. *Married Saints and Blesseds Through the Centuries.*
Translated by Michael J. Miller. San Francisco: Ignatius, 2002.

Popcak, Gregory and Lisa. *Just Married: The Catholic Guide to Surviving
and Thriving in the First Five Years of Marriage.* Notre Dame, IN:
Ave Maria, 2013.

———.*For Better Forever: A Catholic Guide to Lifelong Marriage.* Revised
ed. Huntington, IN: Our Sunday Visitor, 2015.

Retrouvaille. http://www.retrouvaille.org/.
*Resources and programs for healing and renewing struggling
marriages.*

Worldwide Marriage Encounter. http://www.wwme.org/.
Weekend retreats and resources for marriage enrichment.